Praise for
Awakening Healing Axis

"*I love the AHA retreat and workshops. They bring such positivity and love into the world. They help us to expand the depths of our Souls. They teach advanced techniques that stretch our minds to all the possibilities of using the higher frequencies. The healing possibilities are endless for ourselves, others, the world, and the universe. It has created a desire in me to learn even more than the enormous amount that was covered, about the angelic realms, guides and Ascended Masters, crystals, neuroplasticity, our DNA, the physical body, and quantum physics.*" – Penny M-H.

"*Thank you for being the hole in the flute that this consciousness shines through!*" – Jon S.

"*Thank you Jeannette, Franny, and Tim, for a wonderful week of amazing experiences and information. I again have elevated my consciousness and self-awareness to new heights. The frequencies that you bring forward to our collective is beyond description. My heart is open, my mind is clear, and I am ready to move forward with new-found excitement and joy. Thank you for what you do!*" – Michele J.

"*Being a devout student of the Healing Arts for over 20 years, my participation with Awakening Healing Axis has broadened my borders and expanded my insight and consciousness in ways that I have not experienced before. The vocation of being a Healer comes with a personal and universal responsibility to maintain the highest level of self-awareness and integrity in order to serve at your highest potential. Awakening Healing Axis has united an innovative approach and remarkable reverence for their mission to expand on concepts of energy healing.*" – Barbara D.

Awakening

TO HIGHER FREQUENCIES

Awakening
Healing
Axis

A GUIDEBOOK

Awakening Healing Axis Presents

Co-Authors Franny Harcey & Tim McConville

INSPIREBYTES OMNI MEDIA

Distributed globally with Expanded Distribution by KDP.

ISBN Paperback: 978-1-953445-10-0
ISBN E-Book: 978-1-953445-11-7
Library of Congress Control Number: 2021944623

 INSPIREBYTES OMNI MEDIA

Inspirebytes Omni Media LLC
PO Box 988
Wilmette, IL 60091
For more information, please visit www.inspirebytes.com.

AHA Statement

"Our mission is to raise the collective frequency of ourselves and those we support, so that we can aid in the ascension of human consciousness aligned with the highest Rays of Divine Love."

Gifted to Breitenbush Hot Springs

Thank you for this sacred space you hold for so many to replenish and remember their inner light. In gratitude,

Granny

Table of Contents

Foreword
By Cyndi Dale

Years ago, I studied healing with a shaman in the Amazonian basin. He was a spry man for a 70-year-old and loved to play pranks. Once, he stole all our shirts, which had been washed and hung to dry in the jungle sun by village women.

"It's important not to take anything for granted," he grinned, as he passed our half-wet clothing back to us.

He demonstrated healing with many different types of rituals, besides stealth. There was the time he guided each of us to sit in a hollowed-out tree. He then blew curls of smoke at us through his pipe. He said the smoldering fire would draw out our negativity. Maybe it did. At the very least, the obnoxious smell made me lose my stomach toxins. And yet, I didn't really understand the point of his work until I met with him alone.

"Why do you do healing-work?" I queried, thinking he would answer with a bold or mystical response.

"Because of the village," he shared. "I help the villagers to help themselves, so the village can become stronger." He added, "A sound village makes every villager better."

This Iquitos shaman, with his ceremonies, medicines, and special dances, might as well have been reflecting the message presented by Franny Harcey and Tim McConville in this amazing guidebook, *Awakening to Higher Frequencies*. We are each an equally vital member of a greater collective. As such, the whole is only as powerful as its individual members. We can benefit our collective village—the earth, all its inhabitants, and even the cosmos—by developing ourselves. And by evolving the world, our own lives can become happier and healthier.

You've most likely been laboring to improve your personal life. Maybe you've dedicated time to supporting the global community. No matter what you've been up to, unfortunately, we're running out of time. Let's stop concentrating on the negative, and lift ourselves—and this holy world—into the most elevated of heights. The path? It's in this book.

As Franny and Tim explain, the heart of all matter—actually what really matters—is the fact that we're vibratory beings. As Albert Einstein said years ago, there really *isn't* matter. What we see, touch, smell, and the like—what we think of as solid—is simply dense energy.[1] Since energy is information that vibrates, we arrive at the conclusion that all living (and even not living) forms are simply vibration.

However—and this is an extraordinarily important point—there are lower and higher vibrations. Many people spend their time around lower vibrations, which in turn, brings about illness, limitations, and suffering.

The good news is that we're capable of so much more. This is because we *are* more than we appear to be.

We are unlimited beings, capable of raising the frequency of our vibration to wonderfully high levels. After all, we are made of sound and light. Mix that formula with the spark of the Divine that is our essence, and we can bring goodness to all things. If each of us were to commit to transforming ourselves into this type of sacred "villager," the earth would also transform. Its own essence would emerge. We'd find ourselves inhabiting an extradimensional home in which only love is continually exchanged.

Now *that* would be a village we'd enjoy.

---

1. How was the universe created if physics states matter can neither be created nor destroyed? (n.d.). Physics Central. Retrieved from http://physicscentral.org/experiment/askaphysicist/physics-answer.cfm?uid=20120221015143

We wouldn't constantly struggle in our consciousness to decide how to act. Rather, our conscience would take over. As has been said before, a society is only as functional as its ability to care for its most vulnerable members. Compassion and commitment would automatically emerge, along with an increased desire to tend to the children, the needy, and our elders. We'd naturally sustain the waters and land, as well as the animals and plants.

In fact, we'd find ourselves shifting from being a mere "human" by adding the extra "e." We'd be "humane."

This guidebook will get you there. In the process of using it, you'll help get this earth there. That's because it's actually an instruction manual for the embodiment of your Higher Soul.

In order to support your metamorphosis—the raising of your frequency to a higher vibration—the authors first define a lexicon of terms. What is the Soul? The interdimensional nature of reality? The Hara, Vivaxis, sacred geometry, chakras, and the various types of energetic grids that construct reality? The point is made that underneath anything that exists are subtle realms, which the seeker is to be initiated upon.

You're then ushered through one exercise after another, a process that will inevitably activate what I call your "Divine templates." Franny and Tim will help you address everything from healing autoimmune conditions to performing quantum alchemy. Look at the Table of Contents for yourself, and you'll see everything in store!

If you're really ready to become your true self, and evolve this world accordingly, I don't believe this book is optional. It's not one to glance at and put away for a rainy day. It's an education. An instrument. A treatise of sorts for uplifting and upshifting yourself and the world.

These exercises are to be done on an ongoing basis, to support you in following the stages from caterpillar to butterfly?

To assist you, the authors also provide web-based activities, which they lead. This work actually began as heart-based workshops offered throughout the country. As such, the engagement allowed for the transmission of knowledge, not only the learning of data. With the Internet as a vehicle, you can now participate in the authors' events with this book in hand.

In the end, it will all come down—and rise up—to the simple comments made by my shaman friend so many years ago in Peru. We are each called to be a villager, but not just any villager. We are to be that spiritual journeyer that leaves all of life better for our having walked our path.

Cyndi Dale,
Author of 30 internationally renowned books including
Energy Healing for Trauma, Stress & Chronic Illness

Introduction

This book is the first in what we imagine may be a series of works bringing forth higher frequency work. The work presented here represents Awakening Healing Axis' (AHA) thoughts following the 6th in our evolving workshop/retreats. Each workshop focuses on new material, with a noticeable upward trend in energetic frequency. Spirit has nudged us to disseminate this work of raising our energetic frequency in print form, with associated visual teachings.

This is an essential time for all of humanity to awaken and embrace our rapid evolution into a new energetic world. From the beginning of human incarnations, we have been evolving on the path to reunite with our Source. Religious and spiritual traditions have kept our focus on the goal for millennia. Now we are on the cusp of a significant upward shift toward that goal. Many teachers around the globe are bringing in aspects of this leap forward. This work provides essential tools for self-transformation needed to sustain the energetic patterns of this evolutionary step. Once we take those steps to move ourselves to a higher frequency, we can then become the conduit for healing and lifting others.

We had started by outlining the work brought forth in the first of our workshops. But as usual, things change. Our guides then pushed to publish this as the first book and backfill previous teachings. We agree that this level of work is exactly what is needed to aid the collective consciousness of the planet at this particular time.

As long-time energy workers and instructors, AHA began as a triad; we joined each other to create a shift in ourselves and, in turn, those we train. We are often asked what difference it makes if we raise our frequency or vibration. Let us start with clearing up a little language about vibration.

The New Age movement commonly uses the phrase: "raising" vibration. However, vibration is movement and frequency is the rate of that movement. We are actually always vibrating, so we do not really "raise" the vibration. We raise the frequency of the vibration.

Think of it like sound. Increasing vibration (volume), just makes things louder. Raising the frequency (pitch) of sound, however, moves it to a higher note. So, we need to focus on frequency.

If we think about frequency within the context of our emotions and thoughts, lower frequencies are associated with more difficult and less joyful states such as anger, frustration, fear, and negativity. Higher frequency emotions are associated with more positive expressions such as love, joy, hope, and awe.

Spiritually, we are designed to constantly strive for closer connections to the Divine and experience deeper love. This too requires a higher frequency. Therefore, raising your frequency allows for greater happiness and more cohesive interpersonal relationships.

Additionally, many illnesses have a psychosomatic component that has been linked to stress and long-term existence in states of lower frequency. This has been particularly noticeable in the realms of autoimmune disorders. Raising our frequency helps move us into a place of less disease and more efficient bodily function. The benefits of holding a higher frequency show up in a multitude of forms throughout our lives such as: improved health, deeper alignment with goals, more positive relationships, more stable and uplifted mental health, and a richer spiritual life.

We think it is important to have a daily practice of intentionally raising our frequency. Additionally, being mindful of frequency as we interact with others and the world throughout our day is also essential. Most of us cannot hold these higher frequencies without making a conscious effort to nudge it back up as it drifts down.

Higher frequency work is continuing to change those of us who facilitate Awakening Healing Axis in subtle ways. As we are better able to sustain higher frequency, it changes the way we work with clients, teach other energy work classes, and interact with people in our lives. We have noticed that although we teach the exact same curriculum in our old classes, the students seem to be getting more out of them and the work runs deeper. The collective of people that have shared our workshop experiences continue to grow in awareness and are clearly all connected in this work. Spiritually, we sense that we are able to connect at a deeper level and receive greater guidance as our world has become much richer and more expansive. We are still quite capable of experiencing a lower frequency, but we find that we spend less time there and can pull ourselves up more easily.

Though easy to learn, the capacity to shift frequency requires continued practice. It has the potential to change each of us in amazing ways, and the ripples can change our entire planet. We believe frequency shift is one of the keys to human and planetary evolution.

Importance of Science

We strive to respect what we know in terms of current science especially when we expand beyond the known limitations of our current understanding. Jeannette and Tim are both trained in scientific methods and are keenly interested in the scientific understanding of our wonderful world. When referring to scientific principles, we do our best to be accurate within our understanding.

It is also important to realize the nature of scientific study. As a society, we are continually learning new things about our world. If we stop to think about it, we realize that almost all science texts from our college days are virtually useless due to the expansion in knowledge. One generation from now, scientific understanding will have again exponentially increased. How can we possibly state that we completely understand our world, when every day there is a new science discovery in areas we thought we understood?

We need to respect the scientific understandings, yet not let them limit us from exploring beyond those confines. Any good physicist will agree that there are many more dimensions than the 3D view suggests. Various theories predict from 11 to 30 dimensions or more, yet we know almost nothing of these spaces.

Modern science lacks the tools to accurately explore these other dimensions. Perhaps the most sensitive instrument we have available, therefore, is human consciousness and the energy system. Unfortunately, the explorers of these dimensions lack a common vocabulary and rigorous verification and repeatability that define the normal process of the scientific method. As such, oftentimes the science community will scoff at things these consciousness explorers suggest. In our workshops, we do our best to verify and repeat our energetic work, relying on feedback and observations of others. We believe that what we are sensing and describing is not a shared hallucination, but rather a glimpse into the magnificence of our world that has yet to be codified into science books.

How to Use This Work

This work is laid out as a guidebook. That means we will describe how we work and our perspective on the energetic world. Additionally, we offer you guided protocols to use these concepts. The protocols can be used on oneself to aid in healing and personal transformation. They can also be used by an experienced energy therapist to work with clients. We consider this to be advanced work that adds to the skill set of practitioners trained in one or more healing modalities.

When we facilitate this work in workshops, we find the work is repeatable. Our theory is that in the workshop setting, the facilitators model the energetic frequency of the guides and the work. Through the entrainment process, the energy systems of the participant resonates with the frequencies of the facilitator(s).[2] The participant is then able to reproduce those frequencies, once exposed. It does not require conscious awareness on the part of the participant. Their energy system does what is required on an unconscious level.

We have been a little dubious that the subtle frequencies that define the depth of this work can be fully translated via web-based teaching or in a printed volume. We have found that recorded audios and video serve

---

2 Entrainment is defined by a temporal locking process in which one system's motion or signal frequency entrains the frequency of another system.

a respectable role in transmitting and entraining these frequencies. We also realize that only a small number of people have the time, money and priorities required to actually attend one of our workshops.

With this in mind, we will be creating a web-based series of teaching to accompany this book. It is our sincere hope that the combination of printed material and web-based video content will provide the proper combination of material that both satisfies the mind's need for information and the heart's need for energetic connections. We have seen immense transformations in our workshop participants. Our hope is that broader availability of the material can aid many more people in their healing and make a positive impact on humanity.

Chapter One

Importance of
Higher Frequencies

As energy therapy and healing practitioners we are often confronted with situations of chaos and fear. Some more extreme than others but all, nevertheless, tug at our own insecurities and may trigger trauma and/or unresolved personal issues. The question then becomes, "How do we stay afloat in these stormy seas of energies and provide a safe refuge for ourselves and others?"

On the surface, it would seem as if our daily self-care, peaceful life choices, and healing work are enough to fend off the destructive forces of judgment, prejudice, hatred, fear, shame, guilt, or arrogance. This is not an easy nor simple task, especially when confronted by unexpected and/or extreme situations.

The ability to shift our frequency is something everyone can learn but requires continued practice and attention. Personal commitment to this choice can shift each of us in amazing ways.

One of the first tools for manifesting such a shift is discernment. There are many "channels" of energy or energetic radio stations in the energy realms. We are bombarded in our daily interactions with many aspects of the lower frequency channels, much of which is reinforced by social media, marketing, and many of the news headlines. The much more desirable, higher frequency channels, such as "selfless love" and "random acts of kindness" are not publicized as often nor made popular by the media. Thus, it becomes very important to tune into the bigger picture of what is really happening. Good discernment involves asking if this situation or information is of the highest light and whether it should be accepted or ignored.

In the natural world, spring is a time of new energies and perhaps the easiest time to see new beauty in nature. However, we can always be nourished by what nature offers to help keep us grounded and whole. Choosing to tune into nature and a more positive worldview changes our overall perceptions and raises our frequency. Take the time to drink in the mystery of nature's beauty and the inherent goodness of humanity. Awe and wonder can shift our body, emotions, mind, and Spirit to states of bliss and joy, giving us a glimpse of the altered states of the mystics and prophets.

Choose compassion and take the "high road" as much as possible. Media seems to choose the extremes and demonize or falsely elevate people. Everyone is a mix of both good and bad. No one is without flaws. All we can hope for is to act like our better selves most of the time. We are all in this together, and the more we support one another and work as a synergistic team the more we will be able to fuel hope and help maintain our individual and collective equilibrium. In this manner each of us can hold space for the ongoing evolution and ascension of humanity and our planet.

In our collective work, we focus on strengthening and broadening the deepest cores of our human and spiritual existence. This involves high frequency techniques and protocols for transmuting and elevating our abilities to be fully present in this realm, all the while anchored into the core of our earth. This empowers us to stand as conduits for Divine energies of unconditional love, and by fully embodying our Divine light as human and Spirit we have the ability to step into a space of healing at a quantum level. From this place we can help raise the frequency of our clients and others around us to support the healing and enlightenment of all.

Chapter Two

How We Work

Our triad was drawn together in the process of various activities in the Healing Touch Program (HTP) organization. The founder of Healing Touch Program, Janet Mentgen, also serves as a guide to our work as Awakening Healing Axis (AHA). When instructing previous HTP classes we often felt Janet's presence in the classroom, although Janet had left the earth plane. We also sense her presence and guidance in this more advanced work.

As presenters and active members in national and international level organizational activities, we would frequently connect with each other and compare notes about our expanding energetic interests. We found that we were each getting nudged by Spirit to expand the work beyond the envelope of current HTP teachings.

Sometime around 2016, we decided to work together to create an advanced workshop. As the planning unfolded, we realized that this was bigger than one workshop. Led by Spirit, we all said YES, and committed to the unknown by formalizing a business partnership to move the work forward.

We have found the idea of working as a triad to be quite valuable. Discernment is critical in guided or channeled work. The triad organizational model provided the necessary validation checks for each other and also allowed a greatly expanded creativity. Often one of us gets a part of the information and the others can play off it and expand to find what was missing. The old saying "two minds are better than one" seems enhanced by adding a third.

Most of our conversations are via video conference. Less frequently, but more cherished are the times we can physically unite as our triad. The work in this volume is primarily guided work. Each of us receives guidance in our unique way from the pantheon of guides that are interested in serving the advancement of the teachings. Often when we are working with clients, we get guidance to shift the energy in new and different ways. During our times together we may collectively hone the work brought in by one of us or we may bring in new ideas on potential energetic topics. All the new ideas and techniques are tested with willing clients and refined prior to bringing the healing work forward in a workshop.

Often, information comes in swiftly and takes some time to unpack and package in a suitable workshop format. A 20 minute burst of new information can take months to translate into teachable workshop segments. Part of that translation process is to find appropriate real world analogs that can help bridge the understanding.

We believe that it is important that this more esoteric work be woven with current scientific understanding of our world and the physical body. This allows us to understand how energetic work complements medical interventions within the limitations of ever-expanding scientific knowledge.

Chapter Three

Our Early Work

In order to understand our collective, it may help to see where we each came from and how those individual stories join to create the work that is Awakening Healing Axis. We believe that all are on their own path in just the right place. For those reading, it is no accident that you are doing what you are doing and at some level ready for the mystery of what this work may bring to you. The following is each of our stories leading up to the creation of our workshops. [Note: There is a language shift in the following stories from "I" to "we" as each author describes their individual experience.]

Franny's Story

Growing up in Minnesota, my perfect day was being outside communing with nature. I also found great solace in going to church and connecting with God in the way that I knew how to through the teachings of the church. Heck, when I was really young I thought I was going to be a nun one day. One of my greatest spiritual growth times was when I left the Catholic religion behind and followed my heart into connecting with the Divine through meditation and a personal deeper spiritual connection. Mind you, I am very grateful for the base that I received growing up Catholic which gave me a sense of respect for God and the deep connection to the Divine within and beyond.

As a small child I remember "seeing and sensing" the spirits in my parents' home. There must have been a battle of some sort on the land where I grew up, as there were many soldiers that would come through the house. I remember them vividly, but when I reached the age of about 7 or 8, they began to frighten me for some reason, so I adamantly tuned them out and shut off my ability to see and sense them. I don't recall my abilities returning until I was in my late 20's when I had my children.

Visiting my parents' home at that time, I would begin to "see" the same soldiers and spirits that were there as a child. As I began to open to extra sensory perception again, I recall it not being as disturbing as when I was young. It felt as if we were all co-existing in multiple dimensions. I really didn't give it much thought that it wasn't a normal thing for most.

Fast forward 10 years, and in 1999, as I was enjoying my "former life" as a hairstylist, working on client's hair and being in such close proximity with them, I would experience physical sensations such as pain or emotional upset, including tears. I recall thinking I was a bit loopy. I called a dear friend who was an energy worker, and told her I thought I was going crazy as I couldn't stop shaking and crying after seeing a particularly high-strung client. In truth, I thought I was having a nervous breakdown.

My friend advised me to find a Healing Touch class, and since I lived in Colorado at that time, it wasn't a problem. Colorado was the "home of Healing Touch" where Janet Mentgen lived and had her offices. The next weekend I found a class in the Denver area and started my journey. I will be forever grateful for my dear friend Barbara and Healing Touch.

It was there that I found out that I was an empath, and that as an empath I could feel others' pain, emotions, and feelings. Feeling everyone's pain and emotions was overwhelming, and it took me a long time to discern what was mine and what was not. Once I was able to understand the difference, I was better equipped to self-regulate and support my own energy instead of unconsciously taking on someone else's challenges. This freed me up to be a more helpful resource to others. Discernment was the key to helping me create healthy energetic boundaries for myself.

Healing Touch became a new way of life for me. I began practicing the work immediately. It felt as if I was "back home." At that time, I was guided to take six months between each level of the program. I practiced all level 1 techniques for six months, probably seeing 100 clients or more, and I continued this process for levels 2 and 3.

Upon completion of Level 3 Healing Touch, I had the opportunity to begin studying with Janet Mentgen. Janet had an advanced class called "The Path of the Healer" where she would teach and share advanced healing concepts. Janet was an avid student of Alice Bailey and Torkum Saradarian's works. I remember how used and loved her Esoteric Healing book by Bailey was. It was such an honor to be studying with Janet, and I looked forward to each time I would be in the group.

After my Level 4 HT class, I was guided to ask Janet Mentgen to be my mentor. She lovingly agreed and this began a whole new journey for me. At that time, Janet had already been diagnosed with breast cancer, so my time with her would be at her home in Arvada, CO. It was about an hour and a half trip from my home to hers, but it never seemed like a long drive as I knew I would get to be with Janet and learn from her.

Thankfully, I got to be with her two or more times a week for a year until she passed away. I am forever grateful for the knowledge that she shared with me. I learned so much just by being in her presence. With few words, she would intentionally share energetic understandings and concepts with me through her energy field during sessions when she would be on the treatment table. This knowledge allowed me to continue to grow and embrace who I am. This knowledge invited me to bring about healing for myself, each person I met, and ultimately support the collective of humanity by being the light and reflecting others' divinity to them.

After studying with Janet, I also had the opportunity to study for four years with Rev. Rudy Noël. (Rudy shared the Mind Clearing and Hopi Techniques that are taught in the Healing Touch Program.) Rudy and Janet had collaborated many years earlier, and through my connection to her, I met Rudy and he shared his knowledge with me as well. Rudy always invited me to explore the "inner world of Franny" so that I could be the light that I am meant to be. He had such a joyful way about him that reminded me always to smile, be self-compassionate, and ever the child within.

Over the course of more than two decades, I have studied with other great healers and feel very blessed to have been present with so many at the time that I was, so that I could embrace many different ways of being, learning, and bringing forth healing work. I studied shamanism, the akashic records, HT animals, mind/energy/body transformation, among other things. All were a new tool to add to my toolkit to support me in the continual opening to the gifts I have and why I am here on the earth at this time.

I started my healing practice shortly after my Level 1 HT class, accepting donations to purchase a treatment table. Since then, I have had the honor of working with thousands of clients over the past 20 years. In the past six years, my practice has evolved to mainly distance client sessions, which has allowed me to travel and facilitate workshops and retreats which is a great passion for me and has contributed to the evolution of my being and my practice. This, in turn, has also supported me to share deeper levels of consciousness and guided work with clients.

One of my great passions is mentoring others in the healing arts. I have been blessed to be able to mentor many energy workers that are exploring who they are and how to be the best that they can be, first for themselves and then for the family, friends, or clients they work with. It is such a great joy to continue to reflect each one's Divinity back to them as they each embark on their inner growth and own healing journey.

In 2013 (with much spiritual guidance) I brought forward a technique in working with the back sides of the chakras (Back Chakra Activation). Having taught this throughout North America numerous times, it gave me a sense of the desire I had to bring more advanced work forward. This desire and passion allowed me to say "Yes!" to creating the Awakening Healing Axis with my wonderful colleagues.

Tim's Story

I have spent much of my life as a seeker. Raised in a good Catholic family of ten children, I was familiar with prayer, rosary, and faith. I was an altar boy for years, regularly helping with funerals, weddings, and daily masses, but by adolescence, I yearned for more than the Catholic teachings were offering. And yet, I am thankful for that mystical aspect of Catholicism that became part of my mental fabric. As a child I remember reading about yogis, saints, and other spiritual giants, and I considered myself a closet mystic. My path evolved from there over the course of my life.

Once out of college, I began reading voraciously about all things metaphysical, participating in meditation groups and dabbling in some healing work. In the early 1980s, I scoured the libraries for virtually every book I could find on metaphysics and non-Christian spirituality. At some point I realized that what I was looking for could not be found in a book. I had followed Yogananda's writing as well as Sai Baba. I made a few spiritual trips to India spending my time in ashrams and studying Vedic spirituality. I had also taken a couple levels of Reiki in the 1990s, however, I didn't really dive deep into healing work until my 50th year.

As a manager and VP in a Consulting Engineering Firm, I was reluctant to share my deeper interests publicly. My work world was full of scientific thinkers that tended to be skeptical about things that could not be measured. I, too, struggled internally as my engineering training taught me to trust the scientific process. It took a couple of personal experiences to convince my engineer brain that the energetic world is truly real.

The first experience happened before I was trained in healing practices. It occurred after a serious motorcycle accident incurred by a family member. He was in a coma for weeks at a local hospital, and I would periodically visit and meditate with him. I found it rather amazing to watch his vital signs on the hospital monitors as I did my meditations. I could literally see the positive shifts on the monitors. At last, I found something I could measure!

Another formative experience prior to healing training happened in a meditation group. A member asked for healing as they were losing their ability to hear. I was asked to place my hands over her ears while the other 20 or so meditators focused on her healing. As I stood there with eyes closed, I distinctly felt an extra pair of hands cover my hands and a surge of energy flow through my hands. I opened my eyes to realize only my hands were there, but the surge of energy and sensation continued. The recipient later reported an improvement in her hearing. These profound incidents quieted the doubt in my mind and encouraged me to explore deeper.

Tired of the constant travel, I quit the consulting business and took other engineering jobs that allowed me more time with family and even a chance to volunteer more in the community. I found volunteering at a crisis nursery helping the children very rewarding. Who would not enjoy rocking babies! Serendipitously, one of the nearby hospitals was starting an Integrative Medicine Department and for some reason that piqued my interest and I felt drawn to volunteer.

When I called them about their program, I was told that Healing Touch training would allow me to volunteer. So, I signed up for the next level 1 class available. Almost immediately, I was smitten. I began to practice Healing Touch with family, friends, and everybody that would say yes when I asked to practice on them. The hospital rules required that I wait until taking the level 4 class before I could volunteer, so it was another year before I could join the hospital.

For four years, I volunteered, working with patients on the hospital floors until I began teaching HT classes there and moved into a part-time job doing research for the Integrative Medicine department. At the same time, I was also volunteering my healing services at a senior center. I still see some of those early clients 15+ years later. I have also maintained an active volunteer position at another hospital for over ten years now. I found that the mix of volunteer work and a paying client practice has worked well for me in my semi-retired mode.

I began teaching Healing Touch classes in 2007. Shortly thereafter, I dropped out of the corporate world and started my "early retirement." The reality is that I am anything but retired. I am just as busy now with a variety of healing activities as I was when I was working as an engineer. Fortunately, my wife and partner Pam also developed an interest in healing work, and she handles the organization and coordination of our classes. She is a partner in our mentoring work as well. With Pam's help, and support from many other individuals, we have been able to continually build a local community of healers.

We began our international teaching efforts in 2013. An instructor was needed in Nepal to help train the local instructor to advance. I agreed to go in the spring that year and taught three classes. We returned in

2015 to hold classes, just prior to the big earthquake. We found those trips to be quite rewarding. As we have found, healing work transcends language and cultural differences, and the people we met and worked with were quite open to receiving.

After our Nepal trip in 2013 we decided to try teaching in Sweden. Since our daughter lives there, we spend a lot of time visiting family and doting on our grandchildren. In the fall of that year, we started out with a two-hour introductory class. Somehow during that class, the words came out of my mouth offering a session to everyone that wished to try. One of the local psychologists offered her office for the experiences, and of the 14 people in attendance all but one wanted a session.

I gave full one-hour sessions to everyone. It felt somewhat surprising at the time, because every single session was profound and amazing. I thought to myself "something is happening here and the timing must be perfect." I had never had such a high rate of interest, nor had I ever offered sessions to everybody. The people from the first introductory course are now the foundation of Stockholm's Healing Touch community. One of them is our local coordinator and maintains a Swedish web site and Facebook page.

Suffice to say, the journey of teaching and practicing Healing Touch has been amazing. It is so rich with rewarding moments of deeply touching and helping thousands of people. I have long lost track of the number of people it has profoundly helped, yet I count myself among them as Healing Touch has greatly deepened my spiritual journey, opened unseen doors, and given me joys I would not—and could not—have imagined before. While I find Healing Touch to be amazing and know that it provides a wonderful foundation, I also realize that it is one of many different healing modalities, and my curiosity has led me to explore other modalities through both experience and reading.

One of the modalities that I explored was Cleansing Flow, and I took one of the first classes offered in this modality. That first morning in class I had a distinct knowing that I was supposed to be involved with this teaching. I told the instructor, and he said he also knew that I was to be part of the work. Both of us had no idea how that would play out, and we both said "yes" to Spirit. As a result, I worked with the organization as they developed the work and became their next instructor.

The work was initially focused on autoimmune diseases, but later expanded into other niches.

My time focusing on Cleansing Flow was instrumental in deepening my trust in working with guides and the Angelic kingdom. I came to realize and trust that everything I did was heavily guided. The more I trusted, the more profound the work became. I came to realize that I was just a bridge and the spiritual essence of my clients and Spirit world were really doing all the healing work. A perfect example of this trust happened when I was in Denver one weekend, coming back on a Monday morning, with clients scheduled for the afternoon.

Our airport shuttle was stuck in a traffic jam on the way to the Denver airport. I was in the front of the bus and listened as the driver called dispatch looking for options. He was told there was no other option but to stay the course. Knowing that decision would result in a missed flight, I closed my eyes and went within. I said to my guides "you have clients this afternoon, you need to get me to the airport." Almost immediately, a fellow from the back of the bus came up to the driver and instructed him to go on the shoulder to the next exit. The man proceeded to guide the driver through back roads to the airport in time for me to catch my flight. I think my guides used that opportunity to show me that they are there for me at all times and that I just need to directly call on them.

As my healing and teaching practice—and trust in guidance—grew, the unseen guides would show me different techniques to use for healing. I would keep notes on the things they taught me and share them with some of the others in our healing community. At first it was simple things. Then the things they showed me became more elaborate and complicated. I would puzzle about the need to go into such detail when just asking for grace and healing often gives good results. Eventually, however, I began to realize that the level of detail also allows for a deeper level of intentionality and shared work with the guides. The Extradimensional Grid work is an example of this more complicated sequence. (We may detail it in a later book as part of the first Awakening Healing Axis workshop.)

Originally, I struggled to name it until I finally just sat down at the keyboard and let the guides pick out the letters. The treatment session came to me in pieces and was modified as I tested it with multiple clients. When the protocol stopped changing, I felt nudged to teach it as a class. After dragging my feet for some time, I finally put the materials together and promoted it as a one-day healing technique class. Over 20 people came to that first class in Minneapolis and the material was well-received. This teaching was taught elsewhere and became one of the vehicles and foundational elements that allowed me to say "Yes!" when the idea of working with our AHA triad began.

About Jeannette

Since childhood, Jeannette's curiosity and intuition have resulted in many journeys of exploration. Her passion for wanting to know more led her to study the major fields of science and resulted in a fulfilling career for 35 years as a secondary teacher and athletics coach. Her sensitivity to energy, on the other hand, guided her to study spirituality and for many years she strove to find ways to integrate science with energy medicine. Eventually she found the Healing Touch Program.

Jeannette's conceptual clarity with respect to both theory and technique is pivotal to her goal of empowering others. Her continuous exploration and training in many different modalities, including Reiki, Crystals, Angel Therapy, Mediumship, and Mysticism, is further supported by her study of yoga and all things esoteric.

What Jeannette brings forward is part of the fusion of this work and is vital to Awakening Healing Axis. As we continued to work collaboratively, her input has helped shape the workshops and hence the content of this book. When the idea of sharing our work in written form developed, her schedule could not take one more task. Since Jeannette has taken on other responsibilities, she stepped away from co-authoring this book but continues to be a key figure in our collaboration of all other AHA works.

Chapter Four

Creating Our Triad

In 2006, Franny and Tim met at a Healing Touch (HT) instructors' training. Two years later, Jeannette took the instructors' training where she met Franny. Subsequently, Jeannette met Tim while working together on the HTP certification committee. Looking back, it seems clear that our trio was destined to meet and come together.

From about 2009, the three of us worked together a few times a year energetically on different supportive projects. In working to support the collective, we found that we enjoyed our time together in the energetic realms. We began collaborating more consistently with new ideas coming forward from guidance for each of us, individually. As we spent more time together, our connection grew stronger and the collective guidance urged us to work together.

In 2015, we began meeting regularly via phone. This evolved to video conferencing twice a month, and by late 2016, we decided to create a collective work to bring forward to the public in order to share our guided joint information. In the fall of 2017, we hosted our first retreat together in Colorado Springs, Colorado.

We continued to collaborate as a collective bringing the work forward with new material for each retreat which have been held twice a year at different locations ever since. We have also created and facilitated 1-day workshops throughout the US and Canada during this time.

Some of AHA's work that has been brought forward that we intend to be the subject of additional books embrace the following topics and concepts:

- Esoteric Healing
- The Science of your Biofield and the Impact On Healing
- Limitlessness of Your Soul
- Expansion of Multidimensional Healing
- Extradimensional Clearing
- Advanced Back Chakra Activation
- Soul Contracts and the Incarnation Grid
- Organ Transplants, Amputees and Surgical Replacements
- Working with the Energy of the Scalar Wave
- Experiencing and working with Different Frequencies of Color and the Elements
- Enhancing your Ability to Guide Self & Others from the Heart
- Enhancing Multidimensional Healing with Sacred Geometry
- Biofield and Biophotons (Lighting Up Your Cells)
- Illuminating the Quantum Fascia
- Claiming Your Heart's Note / Sacred Toning and Embracing the Collective Symphony
- Core Essence Expansion and Elevation: Living as Divine, Moment to Moment
- Growing, Expanding and Transforming Your Gifts as a Healer
- Healing Autoimmune Conditions
- Exploring your Extradimensional Quantum Existence
- Joyful Communion with your Essence and the Divine Collective
- Quantum Alchemy
- PTSD and Transgenerational Trauma.
- Chakra Fusion
- The Power of your Heart: Embodying Esoteric Healing
- Nurture your Intuitive Gifts

Chapter Five

Energetic Framework

To really access the work in this book, it is important to first understand our viewpoint of the unseen aspects of the human energetic system. This understanding both informs the work and assists in directing the intentionality of our protocols.

We believe our existence on this planet is far more complex than the physical and mental framework often portrayed by scientific understanding. Our existence and interactions with others are a multidimensional experience. The understanding we offer is built upon the teachings of many mystics and explorers of this area. Over time, our guides have continued to expand our understanding of this framework. If you have studied this subject widely enough, you are probably aware that there are inconsistencies in terminology and differing explanations.

We liken this phenomena to the old story of a group of blind men describing an elephant as they touch different parts. Each may be correct yet provide only a partial view of the whole.

Just like the blind men in the story, we are limited in the ways we experience the world beyond our five senses. Each of us—each energetic explorer—has different gifts to experience the unseen. All may be correct, but all are still limited to the gifts of the seer. So, what happens when we are faced with the significant issue of our human desire to linearize and fit the multidimensional universe into a 3D box? It simply doesn't work. It would be akin to making two dimensional drawings of ten dimensional objects, just so it fits in a book.

Therefore, the following is our attempt to describe our current and ever-evolving understanding of our energetic framework. In offering this information, we acknowledge that our limited human minds are only marginally capable of accurately understanding and translating the infinite into the finite. Again, like the blind men, we can report what we see with accuracy, but the true scope of the whole still resides mainly in the mist.

Core Essence

We think of Core Essence as our true self—our fundamental multi-dimensional spiritual being that we are. This is the purest aspect of who we are and is in resonance with the oneness of everything. At this level we are pure and untainted by the trials and tribulations of living on earth. This aspect of our being is never harmed and never traumatized. Core Essence exists in a different dimension. This highest frequency of our spiritual being cannot be fully experienced on the physical plane. Just as electricity is stepped down from high voltage lines by transformers to household current levels, our Core Essence gets stepped down into the lower frequencies of our existence in order to manifest on the physical plane.

We consider Soul to be a subset of Core Essence. Soul seems to hold more earthbound characteristics. Perhaps Soul is more like the level of consciousness needed to bridge the dimensional realities and manage our lessons while on the earth plane. Our concept of Core Essence is similar to what Barbara Brennan described in her book, *Light Emerging*, as Core Star in her work.[3] Her visuals of Core Star show it as located in the middle of the body, just above the navel. That may have been generally true in 1993 when her work was published. Visually identifying these aspects within our physical self is a useful tool that helps our limited minds work with these concepts.

Keeping in mind that Core Essence (or Core Star) is a higher dimension of self, our concept of Core Essence allows it to be more fluid, which can make it appear higher in the physical body

---

3 Brennan, B. A. (1993). *Light Emerging; The Journey of Personal Healing.* Bantam Books.

as people increase their energetic frequency. In fact, humanity's collective evolution is allowing Core Essence to be moved higher and higher. Our work encourages that elevation, with the goal to raise it out of the space of physical manifestation, into our spiritual energetic layers.

We sense Core Essence to be a quite malleable part of our energy self. It can be expanded, contracted, and elevated as one learns to master and better regulate the expression of their energetic being.

The Hara

Our understanding of the Hara is rooted in the work of Barbara Brennan. We believe that channeled work from the 1990s is a good foundation, however we are constantly evolving in an energetic sense. Therefore, it is best to see the earlier work as a good introduction, realizing that we may now be different in subtle and important ways. The Hara exists in the dimension of intention. Decades ago, Brennan's work suggested that it was the 4th dimension. Our guidance now tells us to simply say another dimension rather than labeling any particular dimension.

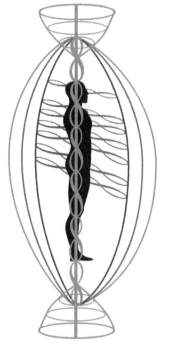

Defining the Hara requires an understanding of the concept that our intention to incarnate on planet earth manifests an energetic connection between our Core Essence and the earth. That energetic connection is held in place by the intentionality of being incarnate and becomes the basis and foundation for our physical and energetic bodies. Although the Hara is probably a multidimensional holographic projection, Brennan's description is much easier to understand.

The Hara begins to take form with the intention to incarnate, which means it begins to manifest well before our birth. In our work, we have sensed an incoming child's energy system well before conception. The Hara, therefore, is a line of energy connected to the core of planet earth. Along that line of energy there are three aspects of the Hara: the Tan Tien, Soul Seat, and Point of Individuation (ID). The Tan Tien is located in our lower abdomen. The Soul Seat is near the thymus gland, and the ID point is located at a point above our head where the aura starts. Keep in mind that the Hara is another dimension so it will not be physically found within the body.

The Hara becomes the foundation of our earthly energetic system. Brennan also describes Hara as carrying a unique specific sound note or frequency. That unique individual frequency is part of the definition of who we are on this planet. Our chakras and fields then develop around the Hara, and each of the three aspects of the Hara have certain characteristics.

- The Tan Tien carries the note and makes the physical connection to the Hara. The Tan Tien is used extensively in martial arts training.

- The Soul Seat holds our spiritual longings and desires.

- The ID point holds our connection to Spirit or Divine energy.

As the Hara holds our intentionality to be on earth, it also contains a connection to our life's purpose. The stronger and more aligned one's Hara, the better the realization and alignment to life's purpose. Subsequently, if one's intentionality to be on earth is not clear, it will energetically appear as some level of distortion in the Hara.

Brennan described the Hara as a laser line of light, and many carry forward that visual of a very thin Hara line. However, it is our experience that the Hara can be much wider. Perhaps it is due to evolutionary shifts in our energy structure over the last few decades. Our perspective is that a wider Hara can carry more energy. We often use the metaphor of a garden hose versus a fire hose. The larger hose allows much greater flow of water, so a larger Hara allows more energy flow. That said, we also caution that one needs to be able to regulate and control the amount of energy flow. Bigger is not necessarily better, if you can't properly use it.

We have been slowly increasing the size and expansion of the Hara that we teach in our work. One must slowly increase the size as they learn to regulate and control the extra energy. At a recent workshop we had participants expand and experience an increasingly wider Hara, with instructions to bring it back to what felt right after experiencing the expansion. There were several reports of people then having tripped circuits and other electrical issues with the technology devices in their life. One even reported a light that would not go out, unscrewing the bulb and having the bulb still glowing in their hand. Although amusing, such dysregulation is not very practical for living in our normal 3D realities.

The Hara has structure, both internal and external. We sense the outside structure of the Hara as a woven pattern with the weave patterns spiraling in both clockwise and counterclockwise directions. Similarly, there seem to be internal structures of opposite spirals, much the way Kundalini energy is often depicted.

The Hara can be distorted in a wide variety of ways. Some distortion can be related to past life trauma or lack of clarity in the intentionality of incarnation. Traumas in this life can also impact the Hara, causing leaks, tears, or distortions. A healthy Hara should be straight like a column of light. Some distortions may cause it to tilt at an angle either above or below, limiting

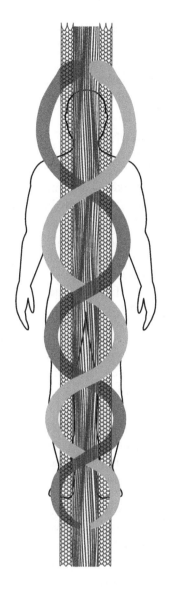

connections to either earth or Source energies. Leaks and tears in the Hara may limit access to full energy flow and can ultimately lead to disease or illness. The Hara can also become weak and poorly defined when intentionality to be on earth wanes. We have seen this at the end of life or even in children that are struggling with life on earth, having recently reincarnated.

The Hara, like all aspects of our energy structure, can be healed, upgraded, and repaired with the help of skilled energy workers. These helpers could be incarnate or in the spirit realm. Our work includes practices to repair and keep regular energetic hygiene of our Haras and also helps our clients do the same.

The Vivaxis

The Vivaxis and the Hara are completely different energetic structures and likely exist in different dimensions. Both are equally important but in quite different ways. The Hara begins sometime before conception or during our time in the womb, whereas the Vivaxis energetically makes a connection near the time of our birth. We choose to incarnate into a specific family in a certain physical location for our lessons in earth school. The Vivaxis is a specific connection to the earth that you anchor into at that location on the earth where you choose to incarnate.

We create a little energetic sphere that anchors in and to the earth and connects to us as we move around, like a virtual cord. It stays anchored there throughout your lifetime unless it is intentionally moved to a different location. This cord allows energy to flow, completing a circuit between the earth and ourselves. Our bones and fascia are the chief carriers of our Vivaxis forces. The Vivaxis is an anchoring force to the earth. When clear and flowing, the Vivaxis feeds us with minerals and nutrients from the earth. This flow is on a frequency level, and does not actually transport minerals physically.

We sense this flow of energy via the Vivaxis coming into the body up the left leg. We sense it quite strongly, almost like a hose in the lower leg and bones. As it moves up the leg it begins to disperse into the fascia tissues as well. It continues up the body crossing the heart to the right side, then moves up around the head from right to left. It then flows back down crossing the heart again and exits the body along the entire right side. We find it more difficult to sense the return flow on the right as it is much more dispersed than the concentrated flow coming into the body.

We have also become aware that the Vivaxis is somehow energetically interwoven with the 10th Chakra. We do not sense that the

Vivaxis flow is through the 10th Chakra, however. It seems that changes in the Vivaxis interact with and affect the 10th Chakra. That interaction could be in the quantum relationships of all aspects of our energy system.

The primary focus of our Vivaxis work is to help people reestablish and maintain healthy Vivaxis connections. Prior to joining together, each of us had dabbled with the concept of Vivaxis connections and was aware of the books on the subject. However, it was not until we were working in the AHA triad that we began to understand the importance of the Vivaxis. We recommend reading *The Vivaxis Connection* by Judy Jacka, ND, who had studied Fran Dixon's work intently. Again, we see this early work as a good foundation, although we have a somewhat different sense about certain aspects. Jacka also goes into a great amount of detail about the chemical aspects of the Vivaxis, which we have not felt drawn to explore yet. We feel that this would be a great area of exploration for someone that focuses on energetic rather than product-based approaches to micronutrition.

Our healing work includes sensing and working with the Vivaxis. As healers, it is important that we do our self-care work and maintain a healthy Vivaxis. When assessing our own or a client's energy system, the Vivaxis is an important element to check. We usually do this while standing at or holding the client's feet, when working locally. When working remotely or for self, we just tune into the flow of energy in the Vivaxis.

To do this, the first step is to feel into the Vivaxis flow at the left foot to assess the connection. Then, focus on the energetic sphere where the Vivaxis connects to the earth. It is possible that the sphere is not functioning properly or is not integrated into the gridwork of the earth at that locality. Sometimes it appears the sphere is just dormant. When assessing and working with the sphere, again ask for help from Spirit. Visualize the sphere as radiant. Ask that the energetic structure of the sphere be upgraded and allow it to fuse and integrate with the highest frequencies of the local earth matrix.

For many people the Vivaxis has just become sluggish and less effective, analogous to a pipe that has become clogged and corroded. For those cases ask the spirit helpers to help shift the Vivaxis flow to its optimum function at this time. We often envision iridescent colors flowing into the Vivaxis as it is cleared and restructured.

Unfortunately, for some people the Vivaxis does not even connect to the earth. We have seen a few individuals where the Vivaxis seems to float along above the earth not connecting to it, or even connecting to a portal or other dimension. Sometimes trauma related to the original connection, or a distortion of the earth at the original connection, makes it difficult to reestablish a good connection. In some cases, it has been beneficial to move the Vivaxis connection to a more supportive location on earth. Moving the Vivaxis should not be taken lightly and only done with spiritual help and guidance. Additionally, moving it to a place based on ego-related whims may not be in the person's highest good. The work of Jacka and Dixon suggest that the movement of the Vivaxis needs to be done with a physical process. We believe it can be managed by the purest of intention and projection of consciousness.

Grounding

Being grounded in this earthly existence is probably one of the most important—yet least practiced—spiritual disciplines. Although there are many techniques and plenty of teachers with the message, there seem to be few people that put it to practice. The combination of 1) a western culture that overvalues the mental, and 2) spiritual guidance that shames the physical and directs our gaze upward, has created a culture of people living in the upper chakras.

We passionately believe that we are the juncture of heaven and earth. We have a choice to be that bridge between the two, or the gap between the two. To many it seems counterintuitive that to raise our frequency high, we must first connect deeply below. We have seen many times when working with students that the key to accessing the energy of above is to first look below. We suggest that an important part of any healing work discipline is to start with the awareness of being grounded and consciously connected to the earth.

The hard part is to then maintain that connection and stay grounded while experiencing lofty higher frequencies and multiple dimensions. One of the keys to achieving this is practice. With practice, we can spread the awareness of being grounded and in the present moment to our everyday life. We aren't suggesting that it is likely we will stay grounded at every waking moment. Slowly gaining a larger percentage of our day would be an achievable goal.

While being grounded is important in spiritual work, it does have benefits in our everyday activities. When we are grounded, we tend to be more aware of our surroundings. We are more able to see the beauty of nature and the people around us. When grounded, we are also less scattered and more present. Our personal interactions and conversations are far richer when we are grounded and paying attention to others. A great many of those moments of forgetfulness or absent-minded mistakes come from being ungrounded. When we forget where we misplaced something, we probably put it down while our mind was in the past or future and we were ungrounded.

The Chakra System

The techniques we are given and the energetic framework include a considerable amount of work with the chakra system. We initially focused primarily on the traditional seven chakras, but also worked with some of the chakras not contained in the body structure. There is a considerable amount of inconsistent information regarding chakras in the world. A quick search of the internet yielded systems ranging from 6 to 114 different chakras, and there are probably even more ideas out there. In general, our view of the chakra system is similar to the 12-chakra system described by author Cyndi Dale. We suggest referencing her material for a deeper explanation of the chakras. Our explanations below will only provide enough information to locate the chakras and work with them within the broader context of our higher frequency techniques.

Chakras are concentrated energy centers in and around our body. Chakras function as part of our sensory system and regulate energy flows to keep our body functioning at optimum levels. Although the term chakra comes from the Sanskrit term for wheel or disk, we think the torus is a better explanation of the shape of a chakra. The torus is a basic natural shape of energetic structures.

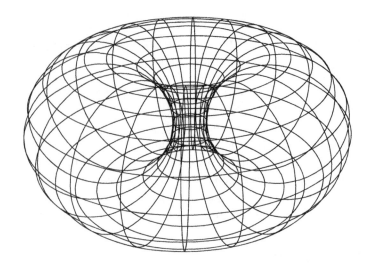

Examples of toroidal energy flow are exhibited throughout nature from the largest galactic structures to the tiniest biological functions, and even smaller. This is the shape that concentrations of electromagnetic energy take. Viewing chakras from this natural perspective also validates both of the common viewpoints that chakras look like disks or that they look like cones. It just depends on the viewer's perspective.

The following is a brief description of each of the chakras. As previously stated, there are many excellent books that describe aspects of the chakras in depth, so we don't feel the need to repeat that information.

1st – Root: Located at pelvic floor; Red
Front aspect: This is our basic primal survival chakra (tribal). It is instinctual and about our physical health and presence on the planet.
Back aspect: Holds keys to our unconscious beliefs about deserving physical life and well-being, as well as regulates the physical system and flow of universal energy.

2nd – Sacral: Located just below the navel; Orange
Front aspect: The expression of feelings and creativeness with the world. Our connectivity to all others and our sexuality.
Back aspect: Supports the unconscious template of the front side. Supports us through changes and adaptations.

3rd – Solar plexus: Located at solar plexus; Yellow
Front aspect: The source of our self-esteem and self-power, our ability

to succeed in the world. Our thoughts and mental structures.
Back aspect: Our mental templates of self and how the world works.

4th – Heart: Located at center of chest, near nipple line; Green
Front aspect: Love and abilities to give and receive with others. Heart balances the lower and upper chakras.
Back aspect: Connection to our heart's desire, unconscious belief about love and relationships with others and the Divine.

5th – Throat: Located at base of throat; Sky blue
Front aspect: Expression, communication, and creativity. Alignment of will and guidance from Spirit.
Back aspect: Access point for external spiritual guidance.

6th – Brow: Located at center of the forehead, just above the brow: Indigo
Front aspect: Seat of the mind, dreaming, intuition and wisdom. Connection to higher levels of compassion and connection of all humanity.
Back aspect: Our potential and access to higher wisdom and vision.

7th – Crown: Located on top of the head; Violet
Front aspect: Seat of the spirit and truth. How we project our spiritual beliefs and programming. Connection to "knowing."
Back aspect: Opens us to the Divine, filtered by our belief systems.

8th – Located 1–2 inches above the head; Silver
This chakra interacts with beings of different dimensions and planes of existence. Work through past and future lives and visit parallel or concurrent realities.
Front aspect: Expression of your life purpose.
Back aspect: Patterns of karmic and past choices influencing what you attract to your life.

9th – Soul Star: Located 1–2 feet above the head; Copper
Front aspect: projection of your Soul's understanding of love. How you care for and connect with others.
Back aspect: Your Soul's desires and beliefs about love and the world.

10th – Earth Star: Located several inches to a few feet into the earth below our feet; Earth-tone, brown
Front aspect: Our interactions with the world and natural materials.
Back aspect: Aspects of the natural world you connect with. Ancestral lineages that you bring forward. DNA and epigenetic activations, both positive and negative.

11th – Metallic blue. Dale associates this chakra with the hands and feet as well as muscles and connective tissue. Our sense is that it is energetically intertwined with the fascial system. Fascia is electrically conductive and connected to every cell in our body. As such, it is part of the internet of the body.

12th – Gold. Connects all physical elements into the outer layers of the energetic shell that surrounds us.

The Human Energy Field (HEF)

Our Human Energy Field (HEF) is made of similar torus shaped fields that surround our entire physical body. The common understanding is that the HEF consists of several layers. The most common model depicts seven layers to the HEF, each associated with the first seven major chakras. The idea is that each chakra, as it spins, creates an associated field. Some of these layers are composed of lines and grids (odd numbered fields: 1,3,5,7) and some are amorphous and more vapor-like (even number fields: 2,4,6). This common model is workable, and our experience tells us it is pretty accurate, but only a partial picture.

An inquisitive mind might start asking questions about the other chakras. If there are more than seven chakras, why would only some create fields? Our sense is that our HEF or electromagnetic light body is actually far more complex than the simple model would explain.

Perhaps one way to look at it is the seven chakra and field model helps us to understand how we function energetically as an individual. Once we start looking at how we interact with the multidimensional universe, our Souls, and group consciousness, things get more complicated. In the next section, we will attempt to explain some of these additional fields or grids.

Additional Components of the HEF

We preface this section with the disclaimer that we know our understanding is inherently incomplete and approximate. These additional components of the HEF operate multidimensionally and quantumly. Thus, most people, and certainly we, have a difficult time making sense of it.

The problem is our mental models of the world are built in the three dimensions of space (length, width, and depth) plus the 4th dimension of time. However, physics theories require additional dimensions for mathematical consistency in explaining our world. Various physics theories require either 10, 11, 26, or 33 dimensions for the math to work.

Our brains are not particularly good at conceptualizing things in 10 dimensions, and things really start falling apart as we attempt to visualize in 33 dimensions. Many times, we have come up with models or explanations that we thought captured the ideas we are working with, however, when we run it by our guides for verification, we get an answer such as: "Well it is closer, but still not right" or more commonly: "You are trying to linearize the nonlinear, it is more complicated."

So read what we have to offer and see it as a glimpse into a multidimensional quantum world that is fascinating beyond our ability to comprehend. We sometimes get confused about whether something is a grid (more structured) or field (more amorphous), so some of these layers seem to be both or seem to shift between the two. In the end, however, perhaps it is not so important which one they are, as it is more important to acknowledge their existence. These additional components of the HEF, include:

- The Matrix
- The Incarnation Grid
- The Soul Field
- The Fascial Grid
- Other Organizing Fields and Grids
- The Primary Cell

The Matrix

When using the term "The Matrix," many are drawn to notions influenced by the 1999 science fiction movie of that title. However, the concepts of the matrix presented by the movie have only partial relationships to what we view as reality.

In our thinking, The Matrix is a vast fractal-like web structure that creates and organizes the universe or multiverse. What we think of as the "Grand Matrix" is the organizing consciousness of the Creator that pervades everything in all dimensions. We think of this matrix as carrying the instructions and organizing frequencies needed for every level of creation.

Within the grand matrix there are many submatrices for each level of organization. The galaxy, the solar system, the planet, and each living creature has its own matrix, all of which interact with the grand matrix. The structure of our matrix contains the organizing principles, frequencies, and code to maintain our physical and energetic systems and guides us on our journey in this incarnation.

Our individual Matrix is the underlying structure that holds our holographic projection of Lightbody. When we work with the Lightbody we are also working with the multidimensional interactions of the individual and the grand matrix.

The Incarnation Grid

We work with a grid or field we have labeled the Incarnation Grid. Our sense is that this layer contains organizing instructions and patterns that help us to maintain our earthly activities in alignment with the objectives and goals for this incarnation. Numerous clairvoyants and psychics have detailed accounts of a pre-birth planning process that we all participate in. We enter into this incarnation with an agenda or outline of the people we will meet and the lessons we want to learn. It is not tightly scripted and leaves room for free will and experimentation. This outline for the incarnation is somehow energetically coded into this grid structure.

The grid communicates with our Core Essence, universal energy fields, and group consciousness to bring information and occurrences into our life that are in resonance with the grid's frequencies. Synchronistic meetings, sudden insights, and other supposedly "random" events can get organized through communication with this grid. Life events and thought patterns appear to create clutter or distortions in this grid structure. Sometimes completion of major goals or spiritual openings can create possibilities of new goals or realignment of the grid structure.

When we work with the Incarnation Grid structure it is always with the help of our guides. The guides provide filters or cleaning hoops that we use to "comb" through the grid. Sometimes it feels as if it is just being cleaned up. Other times it feels that a new structure is being added. Greater clarity of this grid allows greater access for us to align with our life's purpose.

The Soul Field

Another field we have labeled and work with is the Soul Field. We have sensed that this field or grid is an organizing structure that mediates the interconnection of body and Soul. Our sense is that there is a quantum level communication connection in the region of the heart and thymus. We term "high-heart" as an energetic structure in the physical region of the thymus and closely interwoven with the heart. We work with this field in the same manner that we work with the Incarnation Grid. Using filters provided by the guides we gently pull them through this field. Here, changes to the field are generally more subtle, but noticeable shifts in the field and connections can be perceived.

Within the Soul Field, we may unconsciously hold Soul fragments of another person, or others may have left aspects of themselves with us. These fragments generally do not serve our highest good. So, as the guide brings the filter in, we can invite all fragments we are holding to be released and returned to their sacred home. Additionally, we may have left aspects of ourselves elsewhere or have given them to another to hold. When the guides bring in the filters, we can invite all aspects of ourselves to return to us that are for our highest good.

Internal Fields and Grids

Most discussions of our HEF tend to focus on fields and these grids appear to be beyond the five senses primarily external or outside the physical limits of our bodies. We also believe there are organizing energetic structures within the body. The generally accepted science theories place responsibility for operating the physical structure with our DNA. DNA holds the instruction set for making all the cellular and molecular components we need to maintain life. However, those theories omit the role of consciousness in the regulation of life.

Fascial Grid

One internal grid structure we work with is the Fascial Grid. Fascial tissue forms uninterrupted cellular sheets from head to toe. It weaves through and envelops every cell, organ, and body structure. The fascial tissue binds together structures, creates compartments to hold and transport fluids, and maintains our physical shape. It plays a role in almost every aspect of bodily function. Furthermore, fascial tissue is electrically conductive and may be the "internet" of the body.

We think that the true nature and importance of fascia tissue—and the Fascial Grid—is only now beginning to be understood by the scientific community. Recent years have provided a plethora of new discoveries related to fascial tissue.

We believe that the fascial system is an internal grid structure that is actually part of the electromagnetic HEF. Fascia may be the primary interface between the multidimensional aspects of consciousness and physical manifestation in this earthly plane. Our sense is that the Fascial Field is communicating with the multidimensional HEF on a quantum level. There seems to be a strong quantum connection between the Fascial Field and the Tan Tien aspect of the Hara.

Tim shares an account of one of his first experiences in sensing a distinct Fascial Field.

> This experience came shortly after my mother died when I was present in the room. My mother's Spirit/Soul had stayed around the room outside her body for a little over an hour after her breathing and heart had stopped. With a small ritual, she moved on, as most Souls do. It was after she left the room that my father asked me what I was sensing. So, I walked over to my mother's body to sense and describe for him what I perceived.
>
> I sensed a distinct energetic field around the body that felt more physical than spiritual; it clearly was not the spiritual portion of her. I was curious as I had never separated this field out from the rest of the HEF in an animated body. A sister that was present also confirmed this energetically.

Then, a few hours after death, as family members were still in the room visiting, my sister noticed an energetic "pop." I checked and the field had disappeared. Whatever was holding that field within the body had suddenly released.

Other Organizing Grids or Fields

Our sense is there are many other fields or grids that comprise our energetic structure. As we evolve and ascend, we will probably gain greater awareness of the existence and importance of additional aspects of our energetic structure.

The Primary Cell

To best convey the idea, we draw on the concepts of a Primary Cell from the works of Grant McFetridge and Cyndi Dale. The simple version of the concept is that at conception our everyday sense of self is formed. All of that awareness is consolidated and encoded in the Primary Cell. Just after conception, the fertile egg that becomes us, starts to divide. After the fourth cell division (16 cells), the Primary Cell forms. This cell stays somewhere in the body all our lives.

The Primary Cell resonates with the vibrations of the universal matrix to keep us in sync with our birth intentions. However, this cell would also obviously be encoded with the genetic makeup from our ancestors. Trauma in this life or our ancestor's lineage can cause epigenetic disruption to the cell. This trauma (past lives, ancestral, and present) disrupts the ability to fully resonate with our Divine plan. These disruptions create epigenetic shifts and can cloud the cell's communication ability and therefore our capacity to fully achieve our potential. Healing of the Primary Cell reactivates its ability to communicate and our ability to achieve our full potential.

When working with the Primary Cell, we find that it can be anywhere in the body, although it is often in the upper body near the heart. Prior to working with the Primary Cell, we take care to elevate our frequency and come from a grounded and loving presence. The process we have used involves holding our cupped hands above the heart area and inviting the Primary Cell to energetically come into our outstretched hands. Rarely is there any resistance from the client's Primary Cell. It usually jumps right into the palm of our hands ready to accept the healing work. In the rare times it is reluctant, patience usually pays off as it comes to realize the safe, loving presence being offered.

We often will sense that the Primary Cell is obstructed by some sort of binding, trauma, or neglect. We have gotten images such as an old sea chest, wrapped in chains and barnacles. Or a cell wrapped in webbing. There are a variety of ways the cell presents, and every once in a while, it is radiant. Usually, however, some level of cleaning and releasing is needed before working.

We ask that all binding and obstructions melt away. Once the cell becomes free and clear, we set the intention to gently move and activate the core DNA of the Primary Cell. Depending on the type of healing protocol being used, we fill it with light and let the specific intentions and frequencies of that protocol do the work. Our intentions are always for the client's highest good and that the Primary Cell is able to reach its full potential.

Chapter Six

Working With Personal Energetic Boundaries

Being aware of our own energy is of key importance to stay in a centered relationship with self and to be in a healthy relationship with others. The first step is self-awareness as every reaction is actually about us and not about the other person. If you get bothered by another person, it is always an invitation to look within and explore what your patterns might be. When we can bring that awareness not only into the mind, but into the body and then the energy system, we can recognize more of our "wholeness." This heightened awareness allows us to release old patterns and adopt new ones.

We each have an individuated energy field. This energy field protects us from the world and yet allows us to be connected with the world and beyond (multidimensionally). As stated previously, we know that the energy field is an unseen aspect of who we are. This aspect regulates the inflow and outflow of energy that supplies the impetus to be fully manifest in physical form. We are energy, and we are physical bodies.

When you can notice how far extended or how close your energy field is in relation to your physical body, this supports a deeper understanding of how you interact with others and how you are feeling inside. Many times, you may pick up on another person's "stuff" if you are too far extended energetically. Whereas, if you "run your field" too tightly or close to your body, you may tend to have less contact with the world around you.

Depending on their environment, sea anemones may become large when feeling safe, then when in danger or feeling threatened, they may "shrink" or pull in their body. It is instinctual for them. We too have instinct and unconscious "motives" or awareness that regulates our energy system. We can support how we are in the world and what we choose to create by bringing our awareness to the conscious level of understanding.

Furthermore, our energy system can be regulated to support us more deeply. You can create less drama and trauma in your body and life as you bring your awareness to the conscious level. Your energy body can serve you just as your physical body can. Developing the skills to enhance and strengthen your energetic being can make life more smooth and joyful.

One of the tools we use in bringing awareness to assessing our own energy field is by placing a small hula hoop on the floor. Step into the hoop and consciously bring your field to the size of the hoop. Begin to notice what you are feeling. Some questions you can answer:

- Did you step to the front or the back of the circle? (Don't move, just notice.)
- Are you feeling safe in a circle this size?
- Is your energy filing the hoop in all directions? If not, where is it different?
- Are you comfortable in it? Is it familiar to you or foreign?
- What are the physical sensations you are having? Do you want to run away, sit down or are you indifferent to it?

Stay in the hoop 3–4 minutes. Write down what you noticed. Now try with a larger hoop and expand your field to the size of the larger hoop. Revisit the questions above; What are you noticing? Stay in the circle 3–4 minutes, and write down all that you noticed. All of this information can support you in understanding how you are comfortable and what size energy field feels safe for you.

Awareness is key in learning how to regulate your own energy body.

We often continue explorations using the hoops. Experimenting with interactions between people when in different size hoops or overlapping hoops can provide additional insights into how you manage your field.

As we work with an awareness of a more expanded energy system or HEF, including all the grids and fields and multidimensional aspects of ourselves, creating healthy energetic boundaries becomes even more important. As we work with raising our frequency, a broader view of connecting at higher levels with our Core Essence, and transmuting trauma within the physical body, we tend to get triggered less and less by others "invading our space."

Chapter Seven

Sacred Geometry and Color Elements

Sacred Geometry is an ancient concept that describes the unifying and organizing principles of geometric and mathematical patterns in our world. The energy of creation arranges and organizes itself in specific repeating patterns. Consciousness or Divine principles create the underlying sacred geometric patterns of life. Each specific geometric pattern has its vibrational resonance or frequency. The frequency of specific patterns can be used in the practice of healing arts. The frequencies of a geometric shape can aid in the shifting and moving of energy, helping accomplish the healing goal, bringing harmony and balance to the human energy system.

This section discusses some of the geometric patterns we use in our healing work. This book is not meant to be a treatise on sacred geometry. For more in-depth details, we suggest finding other sources.

Triads

The number three is associated with the trinity and completion. Three is often associated with wisdom and harmony. Biblically, and still in modern use, we often repeat phrases three times. We believe that there is power in the number three and find our work as a triad is much more powerful and fruitful than working in pairs or singularly.

Merkaba

The Merkaba is considered to be a Lightbody vehicle used to connect with and reach higher frequencies. It is also known to be multidimensional, allowing access to the other planes. It is used as a tool by Archangel Metatron. A Merkaba is based on a series of triangles. Think of it as two entwined tetrahedrons, one pointed up, the other down. Each tetrahedron is a pyramid with a triangular base.

We use the Merkaba in many ways. When working with the earth and land, we visualize large Merkabas bringing in healing energy to shift local frequency. We use the imagery in the body working with the chakras and other healing uses. We often visualize ourselves within a Merkaba while meditating. When we work together, we see ourselves as part of a bigger Merkaba. Our triad becomes connecting lines, forming the base triangle and connecting with Christ Consciousness to form the upper pyramid. Our angelic guides connect to form the lower pyramid completing our Merkaba. This is a powerful sacred geometric pattern that can be used in many ways.

Metatron's Cube

Metatron's cube is a sacred geometry symbol that has many meanings. The name is somewhat misleading in that it is not really a cube per se, but a geometric pattern that holds all underlying platonic solids. These shapes combine to create all geometric patterns of the universe.

The shape of Metatron's cube begins with the geometry of the flower of life. To draw the cube in 2D, take the inner 13 circles of a flower of life pattern and connect the centers of all the circles with straight lines. Those lines create the outline that we think of as the symbol of Metatron's cube. In 3D, the cube becomes more complex and contains within it all other platonic solid 3D shapes.

This symbol has long been a sacred symbol in Judaic and then Christian artwork.

There are many interpretations of symbology of this shape, which is said to symbolize the flow and balance of energy throughout the universe. It is used to represent the archangels, alchemy, magic, balance of masculine/feminine, and much more. We encourage the curious learners to explore the meanings and complexities of this sacred geometry by looking to other sources. There has been much written about this shape by authors more steeped in sacred geometry knowledge.

When we draw upon this symbol in our work, we visualize it as a 3D shape, usually spinning. We use the flower of life pattern as a protective shield, and we perceive the "cube" to be a tool wielded by Metatron to clear and heal our energetic systems. We specifically call upon Metatron to use this tool to repair and transmute flaws in our Hara. We visualize this spinning "cube" as a glowing and flashing geometric shape that slowly moves through our Hara, healing as it goes.

Labyrinth

Labyrinths come in many sizes and designs. Labyrinths have been found in numerous unrelated cultures dating to antiquity. The exact uses and spiritual meanings of the ancient examples are subject to much interpretation. Unlike a maze, the labyrinth has a single narrow path from opening to center following a circuitous route to the middle. Much current use of labyrinths is as an art form or an instrument for meditation and contemplation.

The energy concentration in a labyrinth depends very much on the intentionality of its design and construction, the frequency of the users, and the mental state of the individual when walking it. Much like a church building resonates with the collective devotion of the faithful, a labyrinth holds the frequency of its walkers. We have found labyrinths to be useful tools to focus and quiet the mind in preparation for spiritual guidance. The slow meditative walk to the center prepares oneself for an inner journey. Once in the center, we are prepared to open to guidance and communion with the spirit word.

Some of our best inspirations and information have come from sessions in a labyrinth. Franny built a labyrinth on her Colorado property. When creating any labyrinth, careful intentions in building, continued purity of thought, and sacred reverence creates an energetic form that allows that level of spiritual access.

Working with Color Frequencies

Color is vibration. In the color spectrum of the rainbow from red to violet, red vibrates at a more dense/lower frequency, whereas violet vibrates at a less dense/higher frequency, and the other colors range in between.

Each chakra has a color associated with it which, in turn, holds that frequency. We can support our energy system by noticing which chakra may be compromised and bring in that corresponding color frequency to strengthen a particular area.

In 2018, our guidance asked us to begin to work with a higher frequency of colors for the chakras. As we listened, we began to experience the upgraded frequency of iridescence fusing with the chakra colors. Red became iridescent red; orange, iridescent orange, and so on with all the colors. This shifted the frequency to allow for more expansiveness to the energy system.

One of the tools that we teach is to begin to play with colors, to experience them as a felt sensation in your hands and body. One by one, bring each color into your hands and your whole being to experience running different frequencies of color. Sense into the color and notice all aspects of it and how it feels in your body, hands, and being. Hold this color frequency for a minute or more and then switch colors. Allow yourself to experience each color independently before mixing colors so that you have the sense of each color and when it might be used in a healing.

Crystal Grids

Crystal grids are an arrangement of crystal stones aligned in sacred geometric shapes or other alignments that serve to amplify the intentions for healing or manifestation. There are potentially an infinite number of possible grid arrangements. We do not consider ourselves the experts in this arena, as there are many other resources available to help deepen the knowledge for those interested. Our discussion here serves to describe how we have used crystal grids to support our work and in our client practices.

Each of us seem drawn to the frequency of various stones and have plenty of rocks around the house. We find certain crystals or combinations of them to be beneficial for certain clients or situations. We rely on our guidance when deciding to include crystal grids in our workshops and retreats. Some workshops have included grids as part of the protocols, whereas other workshops have limited the use to experiential activities.

Often the crystal grids will be built with a center crystal and an array of supporting stones arranged in a pattern around the center. The center stone serves to both anchor and amplify the frequency of the intention. The surrounding crystals communicate with the center crystal and augment or amplify the center frequency. All crystals should be in alignment and supportive of the frequencies and intentionality of the work.

In the workshop described in this book, we used crystal grids as an evening group experiential. This group activity allowed unstructured "play" time to allow participants to experiment and sense the energetic interactions with the crystals and grids. Through the play they were able to sense how the crystals shifted energy patterns in different arrangements. The groups were able to follow the wisdom of the stones in deciding arrangements. If attention is given to the crystals, they will show you how to arrange themselves.

Half of the workshop participants were participating via Zoom, and it was fascinating to watch how the groups of four, each in a different location, worked. They were able to make grids by "virtually" placing crystals in a grid. The grid held the energetic patterns every bit as well as the grids made by crystals all in "local" configuration.

Chapter Eight

Working With Spiritual Guides

Our experience of the natural world is similar to some of the ideas expressed in the theory of evolutionary cosmology. That school of thought believes that the entire universe is constantly in a state of evolution, rather than in mechanical motion dictated by the laws of physics, and that creative evolution co-exists within the laws of physics, yet is guided by layers of consciousness. Everything exists in nested morphic units, similar to a fractal. Whether it is particles, atoms, molecules, cells, tissues, organisms, societies, planets, solar systems, galaxies, or universes, at every level, things all exist as both a whole and a part of some larger structure or organization. Even respected physicists such as Rupert Sheldrake are finally starting to theorize that perhaps there is guiding intelligence at every level.

Our cosmology follows this train of thought. We believe that there are intelligent forces that guide all aspects of our creation. Those guiding forces, like all matter, are all part of expanding hierarchies of organization and intelligence. All those levels of intelligence can be both the guide and the guided.

So too with us. As co-creators in our world, our spirits are quite powerful, yet we can access far more power if we tap into the vast array of guides at every level of creation. There are legions of angels, guides, and beings throughout the galaxy and universe. We are at once both a part of and the whole of this entire universe. Our evolution as humanity on this planet is deeply intertwined with the evolution of the entire universe. As such, much of the rest of the universe is rallying behind our growth and evolution. As we move forward, so does all of creation. For this reason, we have many helpers at all levels of the galaxy and beyond that are eager to aid if we would just ask.

The following section details some of the many guides that we are aware of that aid in this work. It cannot possibly be anywhere near complete as we are probably only aware of a small fraction of the many levels of guiding intelligences. As our awareness continues to expand, we keep getting pleasant surprises as more benevolent beings are revealed to us.

We want to add a note of caution here. There are many beings and forms of consciousness in the universe. We think of categorizing them in three different segments. Some are benevolent and eager to help humanity. Those in this group recognize the concept that we are all simultaneously both a part of and the whole. With that recognition, our advancement is also theirs and they willingly support this common path forward.

Another segment is in a sense neutral, operating on their own agenda, unaware of our common oneness. They may at times seem to be in our way, but they are just operating on an agenda that at the moment conflicts with our agendas. Perhaps one could think of them as competing for the same energetic resource, which they assume to be limited.

The third segment (we think a small percent) are actively involved in working against humanity. This is as true in the human community as it is in other forms of consciousness. In the human world, we would not willingly share our credit cards with just anyone, only those we have determined will keep our best interests in mind. Much the same as working with humans, one needs to practice discernment when working with these beings.

We have found that the best way to practice discernment is to *only* work with those beings that you have discerned and/or identified are working for your highest good and that of all humanity. This is done by coming into one's heart space, being grounded into the pure earth, and connecting directly to Source. Then, asking if the information presented—or the beings that are bringing the information forward—is of the highest frequency of Divine light. Holding oneself in a high frequency state of being will support in getting an accurate answer.

We would like to make note here that *all* the benevolent beings that we work with are of the Source/Creator. It is our intention to bring forth the Creator's highest frequency of love—the Christ Consciousness light—in this and all dimensions.

Angelic Realms

This book is not meant to be a treatise on the many realms of angels. There are many other resources available to the inquiring reader that define the specific roles each of those groups of angels assume to aid as messengers of the Divine and helpers in this world. Similarly, there are many resources that give expanded details about any particular angelic entity. Note that we do not believe that angels have a gender. They may appear as male or female and we often use a gender-based pronoun, however they are gender neutral.

We are only given a small glimpse of these guides and how they often appear as they offer us assistance. They often show up how we want to see them or in a costume that makes us feel safe. It is our belief and experience that the angelic kingdom is at our service if we would only ask for help. All sincere and altruistic requests for help will be met with an instantaneous response. They seem quite happy to be of service and are honored that we ask for their help. They are bound by this request; however, they must operate within the limits of their rules of engagement and laws of the universe. Angelic and Etheric Beings are not limited by space or time and have the ability to be in multiple places or dimensions simultaneously. They always respect the free will of humans to make good or questionable choices.

Specific Guides And Helpers

Christ Consciousness is the awareness of the presence of God/Creator/Divine at the heart of everything in creation: every atom, being, plant, rock, animal, sun, moon, and all matter and consciousness. We hold to the value and heart-centered knowing that the Christ Consciousness is the purest presence of Divine love, gratitude, and compassion.

Janet Mentgen was the founder of Healing Touch and created a way to bring hands-on healing work to the earth in a more mainstream fashion. Her goal was to have healing hands in every home, school, and hospital. Her strong curricular program created the template of a 5-level foundational energy medicine program for the world. She passed away in 2005 and continues her work from the other side. Janet supports the Awakening Healing Axis collective by being a guiding light and teacher from the etheric realms.

Archangel Michael is mentioned in both old and new testament books as well as the Quran. He is portrayed as both healer and protector. He is often shown with a sword and in cobalt blue colors. We invoke his protection and oversight of our work. He frequently appears in his warrior form, standing guard in healing sessions or when dealing with difficult energies. His softer healing aspect is calming as he infuses that cobalt blue frequency through our nervous system. We see him as a constant companion in this work.

Archangel Metatron appears in Hebrew and Kabbalistic texts as one of the highest of the angels. He had a human incarnation as Enoch before ascending into an elevated status in the angelic kingdom. He is usually depicted with his sacred geometric form of the Metatron cube, which contains all the platonic solids, symbolizing the building blocks of life. He supports our work in a variety of ways, raising our frequency. We specifically call on him to support the transmuting and maintenance of our Hara.

Archangel Uriel is considered one of the major angels in religious texts. Uriel is the leader of the Seraphim and helps with healing resentments and forgiveness. Uriel shows in both gender forms and in red and golden colors. Uriel will step in when called and often appears waiting to be invited for those situations where that frequency can best transmute the stuck energies.

Archangel Raphael is known throughout most Abrahamic religions as the angel of healing. He is one of the archangels always invoked in this healing work. We see him associated with an iridescent emerald green color that can be used to open, transmute, and heal. We often invoke and incorporate the healing frequencies of Raphael's presence into the healing sequences.

Archangel Gabriel has a number of biblical appearances as the messenger of God and protector of truth and righteousness. We experience

Gabriel as a strong protective force and a very soothing energy. Gabriel shows in both gender forms with an iridescent golden yellow light wraps us in warmth, love, and peace. Gabriel heals with a frequency of light, releasing, relaxing, and calming, and is also very useful in calming the nervous system and releasing traumas.

Archangel Raziel shows up in Hebrew texts as the keeper of the secrets and mystery. He is often depicted holding a sacred geometric form. We find him to be quite playful and joyful, bringing in an iridescent frequency of rainbow colors. He often operates as a cosmic level alchemist, transmuting any barriers in multiple dimensions. When we opened to his support, this work shifted into a higher frequency opening new doors. We often ask him to bring in the iridescent rainbow frequencies to clear and transmute.

Archangel Jophiel is considered the angel of beauty and wisdom. When working with us she presents as an iridescent fuchsia frequency. She supports our work in holding a Divine remembering of the beauty and light that we each are directly from Source. Many times, she will appear with her fuchsia mist to surround and bring protection and stillness.

Archangel Zadkiel is considered the angel of mercy and leader of the dominions. He can be invoked as a healer for trauma and mental challenges. Zadkiel brings in the frequency of a deep iridescent indigo blue. He serves with Michael as a leader in battle and captains the angelic Knights Paladin for protection and healing.

Knights Paladin is a powerful group of angels. They appear as male warrior knights. Some of us hear the sounds of their armor as they arrive. Usually, twelve of them appear with Zadkiel when invoked. At times there are more of them. They are a powerful protective force that can be called upon. They are also powerful healers able to transmute in multiple dimensions.

Magenta Warriors and Divine Dragon are a feminine counterpart to the Knights Paladin. They are powerful as a protective force and also marvelous healers. The leader appears often as a feminine warrior, commanding her band of iridescent magenta-colored warriors. They resonate with the frequencies of dragon energy and are amplified with the use of shungite crystals. We refer to the leader as the embodiment of the Divine Dragon energy.

Rahanni are a high frequency angelic and celestial group bringing in the iridescent pink frequency. They are a commanding presence when they arrive. They are great protectors as well as healers. When they are invoked, we often sense them come in suddenly as a powerful column of pink light. When protection is desired, they form a perimeter around the area needing protection. When invoked for healing and transmutation of energy they are softer, yet powerfully transmute the energies and provide sustaining force to enable the healing to hold.

Ascended and Illuminated Masters support the work and the common ascension of humanity and the planet. The Ascended Masters are a collection of guides all having completed their incarnated work on the planet. They continue to learn and grow as they support us all in positions of the spiritual hierarchy. They all have specific areas of responsibility and work with certain frequencies. They will appear as needed and respond when invoked.

Another group that aids the work is referred to by us as the **Iridescent Masters**. This group of high frequency beings supports the iridescent frequencies and helps to maintain high frequency in our personal transformations and healing work.

Many Beings at All Scales help this work. From the atomic level to the galactic level there are benevolent intelligences that are helping our common ascension. At the smallest scale we have been introduced to a group we affectionately label the Comet Beings. These beings zip around at the atomic and molecular level looking like little comets. They seem to come and go as they traverse the multidimensional landscape of the micro level world. They are willingly invoked to assist in transmuting energy throughout the physical body.

At the earth level the cetaceans that roam the oceans are advanced intelligences that support the ascension of the planet and all her inhabitants. They can be invoked to participate in healing work and often transmute energy using sound vibration or toning.

The elemental kingdom of nature spirits is also a resource for healing. They can access many different healing frequencies. As in all things, discernment is especially important with this group as their trust in humans is not uniformly high. They have their own agenda and may not be in alignment with ours.

There are beings and intelligences available at the planetary and solar level that can be called upon when needed. These groups are especially useful when working with large scale energy disturbances related to place and time.

We have also been working with a group we term the Star Beings. They do not self-identify as originating in any particular star system. Their work has been related to bringing in a certain frequency of energy that we sense as a yellow-orange metallic color and high frequency. This frequency is particularly useful in working with the Lightbody and Matrix level healings.

There are many other galactic level intelligences that come to our aid to create the highest frequencies sustainable in the healing work.

Guides and Crystals can work together to enhance the frequency. We have found a number of crystals to be useful to anchor in and amplify the frequencies of the guides. Shungite in particular seems to have opened a gateway into higher frequencies and associated helpers. Our sense is that shungite has been made popular in recent years as part of a grand guided plan to distribute it around the world, enabling a realignment of the planetary grid. The unique crystalline structure of shungite serves well to amplify the frequencies that are being brought in through this work.

When setting a crystal grid, we often start with shungite in the middle and then choose support crystals. Sometimes color is important in the supporting crystal; however, the basic defining quality is frequency. We have used a number of different supporting crystals. Black tourmaline is a favorite along with quartz, varieties of amethyst, more shungite, and several others. The guides asked for several different stones such as anyolite, rhyolite, and dragonstone to support the "dragon" energy frequencies. The yellow amethyst (citrine) supports the "Star Being" frequency. Calcite has also been supportive for the higher frequencies and shifts in planetary alignment.

Chapter Nine

Role of the
Heart in Healing

The heart is the doorway to the love we are all being asked to remember—to remember that we are the gateway to divine re-membering and connection with the Christ Consciousness. In all of our work, we focus on the power of the heart! The toroidal field that emanates from each person's heart expands and fortifies with greater force to strengthen us as humans living within a physical body.

The heart is the bridge between the physical and spiritual realms, inviting us to *be* the love of the Divine here in physical manifestation. It is through embracing the love of the Universe that we may be a clear vessel of light for ourselves, one another, and truly all of humanity.

All high frequency healing is done from a pure heart and divine connection to be a conduit for love to flow through and with us as in-dividuals, working with the highest frequencies of guides and support.

The heart communicates to the brain and body through hormones. In 1983 the heart was reclassified as part of our hormonal system. One of the hormones, atrial peptide, helps to reduce the release of the stress hormone cortisol. So, we have a chemical communication going on between heart and body all of the time. However, this is where things get really interesting. The heart is an electrical organ producing by far the largest amount of electrical energy in our bodies—forty to sixty times as much power as the second strongest source, the brain. This energy permeates every single cell in our bodies. The signal is so strong that it creates an electromagnetic field (Toroidal) that surrounds the body in 360 degrees and can actually be measured up to three to four feet outside the body.

When we increase coherence of our heartbeat, stress levels go down, brain function improves, and we have the ability to feel positive emotions that regenerate us. This all leads to more awareness, intuitive discernment, and the ability to live a more heart-centered life.

Focusing the breath within the body connecting to our heart, mind, Source above, and the heart of the earth, allows us to be present and *be* that conduit for the Christ Consciousness. We strive to hold the template for each person and each participant of our workshops to fully remember that they are here to support themselves and the collective of humanity to bring about the great change we all have the power to contribute to.

Chapter Ten

The Making
of a Workshop

This workshop and all previous and subsequent workshops follow a similar template. We believe it is important to ground our work in scientific principles and earthly knowledge, and to acknowledge the limits of this understanding. We then present our understanding which usually goes well beyond the bounds of currently-accepted scientific thinking. This is important as energetic work can only be partially explained by current scientific models, though it is often more than most people realize. There are also especially useful real-world analogs to energetic practices. Visualization is an important aspect of high frequency work, so it is important that we provide some platform of visualization to more gracefully allow the practitioner to make the leap into the multidimensional space of the high frequency work.

Workshop Preparations

Anyone who has put on a workshop knows that there is a lot of logistical work and planning that goes into creating a successful event. This work requires the same attention to details that any workshop would require. In addition to the usual, we think it is important to take the time to energetically prepare on multiple levels prior to the workshop. We meet a few days prior to our workshops to make sure we have all the materials and presentations ready for the event. We also work to prepare the workshop space and the participants. Well in advance in the planning we "visit" the retreat center grounds in our meditations and together during our phone conversations, preparing the land and working with the energies of the space to clear the area for our work. In the few days before the retreat, we again do guided work to open and clear the land. During our preparations we have been visited by Native American guides that come to help us honor the land.

We also believe it is important to energetically connect and attune with each of the participants prior to the workshops. To aid this process, we ask each participant to send us a picture and write a page or so of background in response to some questions posed about the workshop. We take the time for our triad to sit with each participant's paper and attune with the student. In that process, we get insights into the needs of the various participants, noting that perhaps some subtle energetic shifts were needed. Most importantly we were each more aware of what each person needed and how to be attentive to their energy and interactions during the workshop. We believe that the moment someone commits to a workshop, they energetically link up into the group and at a higher level of consciousness start preparing.

An excellent example was reported to Tim after a one-day workshop. A participant who had never met Tim, said that shortly after she signed up, Tim began appearing to her in her dreams. Over several of her dreams she was given all the information she would receive in the workshop, although she did not realize that was happening. The day of the workshop, she was in amazement as everything we taught was just as she recalled from her dreams. This level of connection and awareness may not be the norm, but we think that it is happening on a subtle level for everyone. We are always connected far beyond our normal level of thinking and understanding.

Labyrinth Ceremonies

We feel that it is important to start and end each workshop with a ceremonial ritual. The labyrinth seems the perfect vessel for that ritual. We always need to work with the local conditions and physical limitations of each labyrinth. Some places do not have a labyrinth. In those cases, we adapt the ceremony, while retaining as much of the energetic characteristic as possible. Unique but similar ceremonies precede each workshop. The opening ritual has more than meets the eye and is designed to catapult the participants into the extradimensional space of the workshop.

As each participant steps into the labyrinth, they step onto the Merkaba symbol and repeat a phrase that opens an energetic door, shifting their energy system to be more receptive to the higher frequency teachings. Of course, each individual shifts in a way that mirrors their personal readiness and openness. Some that are fully ready, are catapulted into extradimensional space, others shift more slightly. As they walk into the labyrinth, the group recites a mantra. Each workshop uses a mantra designed for the energies of that time. Many guides, representatives of the Native American elder's council, and elementals grace our presence and welcome us into the space.

If possible, we have a similar "bookend" ceremony to complete the workshop physically and energetically in the labyrinth. The closing ceremony is designed like the opening. Rather than opening to new concepts the closing ceremony affirms and anchors the teaching. The participants all recite a mantra that is similar to the opening, although it is worded to be a fulfillment and embodiment of the ideas expressed. As they leave the labyrinth, they step on the Merkaba symbol and step out of the energetic envelope that held them for the duration of the workshop. The closing ceremonies are always filled with spiritual helpers, guides, and elementals honoring the light and awakening of all participants.

Sometimes participants are surprised to see how grateful and thankful the guides are. The guides are always eager to be of assistance, but seldom asked to serve as such.

Workshop Experientials

The following two exercises are included in the workshops to allow the participants to experience the power and frequency of forms that would otherwise be merely intellectual constructs. Most of us need to experientially sense something before we can understand it. We have found that this is especially true for energetic sensations that are beyond the normal five senses.

The Merkaba is a sacred geometry pattern, yet many people have no experiential experience with that pattern. The torus is a common energetic phenomena that is part of the human energy system, yet most are unaware of it. These exercises assist to make the patterns more tangible and to anchor an understanding of these energetic concepts.

Merkaba Exercises

As noted in the previous chapters, we consider the Merkaba to be an important sacred geometry element in this work. The Merkaba is much more than a geometric symbol, it is a powerful energetic gateway to accessing and using the higher frequencies available to us. Energy frequencies need to be experienced for us to remember and reproduce them. It is quite helpful to have an intellectual understanding, but it is only through the experiential that we gain the knowing that we seek.

The following describes the exercise we use to allow participants to begin to experience and integrate the power and energy of the Merkaba. Ideally this exercise is done in groups of seven. It can also be done in a group of four, although less effective. Facilitators not only direct the activity but involve themselves in creating the space, directing, and amplifying the flows of energy for maximum benefit. The design of this activity allows everyone to experience the interior energy of the Merkaba as well as be part of creating the energy lines and flow of energy within the Merkaba.

Note: It is important to be aware that occasionally there are participants that find the energy too intense or have difficulty with balance while in the center. Using a chair in the center would be slightly safer; however, it puts the center person at a lower elevation than the rest of the group. We have had only a few such instances in multiple trials with this exercise. Just a note to be aware of such potential. In one instance, a person with inner ear and balance issues could not tolerate the position in the center of the Merkaba and needed to stop. Another incident occurred where the person in the center dropped to the floor, unhurt as they were caught by the group. In that particular case it was actually healing. The energy was so intense that an entity that had been residing in them exited, causing them to momentarily lose balance.

The setup for this exercise is to create groups of seven. Ask one of the group volunteers to start in the middle position. The other six people arrange in a circle around them. Next step is to get every other person to hold hands together, creating sets of triangles. This part can be a little confusing to get people situated correctly. It works best if one person from each of the groups of three is then appointed as group captain to help direct the spin direction of the subgroup.

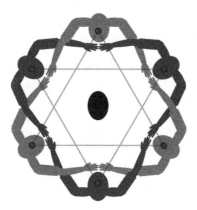

All of the spinning and energetic movement is created on the level of intentionality. The groups are not actually moving during the exercise. One triangle is asked to visualize connecting their triangle of energy with Christ Consciousness above. This creates an upward facing pyramid which they will spin clockwise. The second triangle visualizes connecting below with Janet Mentgen. This creates the second downward facing pyramid, which they will spin counter-clockwise. Once everyone understands their role and energetic assignment, the group is directed to focus their attention on the creation of the Merkaba and spin in the appropriate direction.

This intentionality creates the energetic form of the spinning Merkaba, with high frequency spiritual support. The person standing in the middle of the spinning Merkaba experiences the full energetic power of this dynamic sacred geometry. It is an excellent way to feel that frequency with the full body and get a glimpse into the power and potential. We use Christ Consciousness and Janet Mentgen as the two spiritual ends of the pyramids. Other guides or angels could be used as well. If the exercise is done as a group of four, then three spiritual helpers will be needed to complete the circle of six and create the Merkaba.

Allow the groups to experience the frequency and energy of the Merkaba spinning for 1–2 minutes. Then the group is directed to slow the spin and stop. Switch out the person in the middle. When the switch happens, be mindful of the group captain role making sure each subgroup knows who the captain is. We find it best to switch direction of spin. The triad that was spinning clockwise, shifts to counterclockwise, and vice versa for the other triad. This gives everybody a chance to experience all roles and minimizes dizziness.

Repeat the Merkaba spinning experience for another 1–2 minutes. Continue the process until all seven participants have been in the middle position.

Follow up with sharing of the experience. Everyone will have a unique experience. It is fascinating to hear the different awareness of the energy and the range of experiences that are articulated. This experience creates a building block to energetically understand an element of the frequency shift process.

Torus Experience

We have used variations of our torus experiential as the last workshop exercise prior to completion. Having discussed the torus conceptually during the workshop, most participants have an intellectual idea of the torus as a fundamental shape of chakras and energy bodies. As with most energetic concepts, true understanding is accomplished when we can grasp it both intellectually and feel it with our sensory facilities. This exercise creates a large energy torus with the group which enables most participants to sense and understand the power and flow of energy within the torus.

Creation of the torus is quite simple. The group is divided in half. One half is directed to create a circle, holding hands together. This group will be spaced close to each other. The other group is directed to make a second ring, surrounding the first group. The second group spaces at arm's length apart. This arrangement now makes two concentric circles. Each group is then directed to create a flow of energy in their circle. The inner circle flows energy clockwise (as viewed from above), while the outer circle flows energy counterclockwise. This creates a large energy torus which is usually felt by even the least sensitive members of the group. The feeling is quite powerful.

The experience can be repeated by reversing the direction of flow and noting the difference. The inner and outer groups can also switch places and experience the torus from another perspective.

Chapter Eleven

Basic High
Frequency Shift

We always spend the first part of our gathering focusing on the High Frequency Shift of our energy system. This is an essential part of the work and a recommended daily practice. We believe it is one of the important keys to accessing the frequencies now available on our planet. These energy frequencies are new or have been hidden in recent historical times.

More energy frequencies are constantly being revealed as our human collective is quickly evolving and ascending. At first this may seem complicated as there are many steps to the process; however, with practice it becomes second nature and can be done quickly. When proficient, one can sequence through the steps in just a few moments. When we voice guide meditations for this practice, we typically spend several minutes. It is good to go slowly through it periodically to fully sense and integrate the depth of energetic shifts at each step of the process. One may also realize that the more they practice, the deeper they go and there are many subtle shifts in one's energy awareness. We sometimes feel nudged to slightly modify the order of steps in this sequence, so don't worry if you get them out of order a little bit.

- Invocation/Intention
- Protection
- Hara Attunement/Anchoring
- Vivaxis Transmuting/Healing
- Chakra Opening
- Hara Transmuting/Repair

- Core Essence Expansion
- Core Essence Elevation

Invocation/Intention

The first step is to invoke our spiritual guides. Include your personal guides as well as the angelic helpers. We invite in different spiritual helpers depending on the type of work we are doing. We almost always invoke archangels Michael, Gabriel, Raphael, Uriel, Metatron, and Raziel. In addition to these six, many others will be situationally called upon. It is also important to set the intentionality of the work you are doing, whether you are doing a healing session or just your daily energy hygiene.

The first level of intention we always set is that all will be to the highest good. This overarching intention is important, and it also inherently acknowledges that our conscious minds cannot begin to comprehend what that possibly means. Our limited understanding of "highest good" needs to be put aside to allow for the unfolding of a much grander plan. We may also have some secondary intentions—such as healing a physical or emotional challenge—that we can add.

Protection

The protection step focuses on creating sacred space within and around us for our work. The first step is to envision yourself connected to the Divine Source. How we do that can be very individual as we all have different notions of what Divine Source means. This needs to be your personal connection to "God," the universe, or some higher power. One simple way to visualize this is by having a power cord connecting us to the Divine. Just plug in that cord!

Once connected to Source, we visualize a coating of pure white light that flows over and surrounds us, covering us like paint. If working with a client, cover them with the same protective layers as well. Follow the white layer with a coating of iridescent rainbow colors. Cover that layer with a coating of gold glitter, sparkling all over you.

Next, we bring in an element of sacred geometry. Visualize that you are surrounded in a protective bubble. The bubble has the geometry of the flower of life and shimmers with iridescent rainbow colors. We hold this protection in place as we work with the energy system of ourselves and our clients.

Hara Attunement

Attuning, anchoring, or setting the Hara activates that vertical line of energy that exists in the dimension of intentionality and focuses our connection to earth and purpose in life. We begin by putting our awareness at our Tan Tien, in the lower abdomen. From the Tan Tien visualize a line of energy connecting down to the very center of our planet. Imagine that you have your own personal, exceptionally large crystal in the core of the earth. Anchor that line of energy from the Tan Tien to your core crystal. Allow the frequency of Divine earth energy to flow up your connection, filling your Tan Tien.

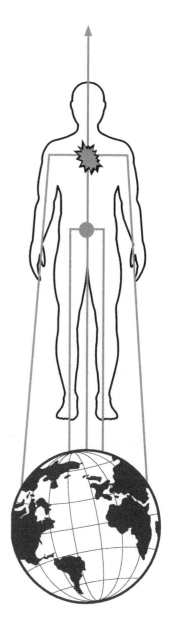

Next, bring your attention to the Soul Seat, located just above the heart. Draw that earth energy into the Soul Seat, then focus on a point above your head and allow the earth energy to flow straight up through the top of your head and connect to the Divine energy of the Universal Source.

Pause a moment to sense the connection to Divine energy both below and above. Visualize a column of light running vertically through you. Optionally, you may focus on expanding and strengthening the Hara connection. Expand by connecting

the energy from the Tan Tien out to your hips, then down your
legs, connecting deep into the earth. Sense your Hara column of
light grow as wide as your hips. Next focus on the Soul Seat,
sending the Hara energy out to your shoulder joints and down
your arms, connecting deep into earth. Pause to sense the feeling
of a stronger, wider Hara now connected by five lines to the core
of the earth and the universe above.

Vivaxis Transmuting/Healing

Bring your attention to Vivaxis. Think of a hose-like connection from
your left foot, off to a place in the earth somewhere near where you
were born. Imagine a small sphere of light in the earth where it
anchors. Sense the quality of that connection and the flow of energy.
Ask your guides to transmute anything that distorts or blocks the flow
of energy in your Vivaxis. Imagine it filled with swirling iridescent
colors of the rainbow or the colors that allow it to flow most freely.
When that connection feels clear and flowing, visualize those colors
flowing up your leg, dispersing into a vapor as they rise up your thigh.

Allow that flow of colors to swirl up across the left hip, through the
torso on the front side, crossing the heart and up toward your right
shoulder. The colors swirl around your head, then down the back side,
again crossing the heart and exiting through the entire right side of
your body, connecting back to the earth. This process may be slower
the first few times you do it. With regular practice you will find your
Vivaxis is normally pretty clear and it goes quickly.

Chakra Opening

The chakra opening step focuses our attention on each of our chakras,
sequentially. This focus opens and clears each chakra, raising its
frequency as it opens. We suggest using the iridescent form of the
colors traditionally associated with each chakra. Starting at the Root
Chakra, imagine a ball of iridescent red light flowing into the chakra,
spinning clockwise. Allow it to fill and energize the chakra, spinning
faster as it opens and clears. Allow yourself time to deeply sense the
chakra open, expand, and shift. Set the intention that it will stay
spinning at that higher frequency.

Bring attention to the Sacral Chakra, visualize an iridescent orange ball of light filling the chakra, flowing and spinning clockwise. Allow the orange light to open, expand, and shift the Sacral Chakra. When it feels full, expanded, and rotating fast, keep it spinning and bring your attention to the Solar Plexus Chakra.

See an iridescent yellow ball of light enveloping your Solar Plexus Chakra, flowing and spinning clockwise. Allow the yellow light to open, expand, and shift the Solar Plexus Chakra. When it feels full, expanded, and rotating fast, keep it spinning and bring your attention to the Heart Chakra.

Imagine an iridescent green ball of light enveloping your Heart Chakra, flowing and spinning clockwise. Allow the green light to open, expand, and shift the Heart Chakra. When it feels full, expanded, and rotating fast, keep it spinning and bring your attention to the Throat Chakra.

Visualize an iridescent sky-blue ball of light enveloping your Throat Chakra, flowing and spinning clockwise. Allow the blue light to open, expand, and shift the Throat Chakra. When it feels full, expanded, and rotating fast, keep it spinning and bring your attention to the Brow Chakra.

See an iridescent indigo ball of light enveloping your Brow Chakra, flowing and spinning clockwise. Allow the indigo light to open, expand, and shift the Brow Chakra. When it feels full, expanded, and rotating fast, keep it spinning and bring your attention to the Crown Chakra.

Imagine an iridescent violet ball of light enveloping your Crown Chakra, flowing and spinning clockwise. Allow the violet light to open, expand, and shift the Crown Chakra. When it feels full, expanded, and rotating fast, keep it spinning and notice how all the chakras are spinning and your energy frequency seems higher.

Hara Transmuting/Repair

We believe that Hara repair is best done by our angelic guides, and Metatron is our "go-to" guide for this work. Metatron uses the tool of his sacred geometric shape, Metatron's cube (previously described), to recondition our Hara from the inside-out. For this step, ask for Metatron's help. Ask that he transmute and repair your Hara to the best condition possible today.

As Metatron does the Hara work, you may experience different sensations as your energy shifts. Sometimes it seems that his cube stays in one place for a long time. This is usually in areas where the energy is not flowing well, and much repair work is needed. Envision Metatron placing his spinning cube into your Hara above the head. As the cube slowly descends your Hara it spins clockwise. As the cube descends you may sense that it moves faster or slower depending on the amount of repair work needed. It slowly works down the Hara column, out below the feet and down to the core of the earth to the crystal where you anchor. Once there, it reverses direction, spinning counterclockwise as it rises through the Hara until it passes above your head.

The cube then reverses direction again and makes a second pass slowly descending and spinning clockwise. The second pass is usually a little quicker as most of the work is done on the first pass. Occasionally a third pass will be needed.

After Metatron has completed the work, invite Archangel Raziel to fill your Hara with a tapestry of golden and iridescent rainbow light, infusing your Hara with the highest frequencies you can hold. Pause and sense your renewed and brilliant Hara.

Core Essence Expansion

The following description is a slower and deeper version of Core Essence expansion. We recommend that you periodically use this slow version as it allows for deeper clearing and heightened sensitivity to the amount of "stuff" we carry in our energy field. We do not need to carry that unnecessary baggage, and we can learn to travel lighter through our daily lives. In our recommended daily practice, you can move through the expansion in a few breaths.

Bring your hands over your heart space. Sense deep within your core being, connecting with your Core Essence. Imagine your Core Essence as a brilliant blue-white star deep in your body. Acknowledge that Divine spark that is your true self. As you focus on your Core

Essence, visualize your star getting brighter and expanding into every cell of your physical body. Feel it light up your entire being.

Using your breath, as you breathe out, continue to slowly expand your Core Essence beyond the boundary of your skin, out into the first layer of your energetic body. Light up and clear your etheric body layer. As you breathe in, imagine your Core Essence drawing back to a point of light deep within. On your next exhalation, slowly expand your Core Essence into the second layer, your emotional energetic body. Sense it light up and clear your emotional body. Let Core Essence dissolve all the emotional energy that you are holding in this body. Pause here for a breath or two, if needed, to fully clear this layer. Be aware of the calmness that comes.

Again, as you breathe in, imagine your Core Essence drawing back to a point of light deep within. Then exhale and slowly expand your Core Essence out into the third layer, your mental energetic body. Sense it light up and clear your mental body. Let Core Essence dissipate all the thought forms and mental energy that you are holding in this body. Pause here for a breath to fully clear this layer and sense the clarity of a revitalized mental body.

Breathe in again and draw Core Essence back to a point of light deep within you. Exhale and slowly expand your Core Essence out into the fourth layer, your astral energetic body. Sense it light up, clear, and vitalize your astral body. Pause here for a breath, if needed, to fully clear and sense this layer.

Breathing in, draw Core Essence back to a point of light. Exhale, slowly expanding Core Essence out into your fifth layer, the etheric template energetic body. This is the blueprint of your physical body. Let Core Essence light up and flow through all the lines and grids of this layer, clearing and vitalizing your etheric template. Pause here for a breath to sense the difference in this layer.

As you breathe in, draw Core Essence back to that point of light deep within. Exhale and slowly expand your Core Essence out into the sixth layer, your celestial energetic body. Sense how iridescent colors flood and expand your celestial body. Pause here for a breath to experience your brilliance.

Finally, as you breathe in one more time, Core Essence draws back to a point of light. Next exhale slowly and expand your Core Essence out, fully expanding into your seventh layer, the ketheric energetic body. Core Essence lights up the golden bubble of energy that surrounds you. Feel your pure full expansion and remember this feeling so you can come here often. Hold Core Essence in this expanded state.

Core Essence Elevation

Elevation of our Core Essence is a key part of accessing the higher frequencies now available. This description is for a slower version which is essential at first and wise to use occasionally if you are able to put this in your daily practice. It has been our experience that once Core Essence is elevated, it is like unlocking access to the frequencies. Core Essence will tend to stay elevated if practiced regularly. If not tended to, it will drift back to our old normal.

Following expansion of Core Essence (previous exercise), bring your hands to your chest, holding them over heart space. Connect into that spark of Core Essence and visualize it moving to your hands. Slowly lift your hands with Core Essence up to the base of your throat, in front of your Throat Chakra. Let it stabilize at the throat and get used to that spot. As you hold your hands by your throat, create the image of a Merkaba in your mind's eye, about the size of your hands, in front of your throat. Invite Core Essence to come into the center of your Merkaba. Your Merkaba is the vehicle for elevating Core Essence.

In the palm of your hands is a beautiful Merkaba with your brilliant Core Essence in the middle. Slowly raise your hands up your face until they are in front of your Brow Chakra. Allow Core Essence to resonate with Brow Chakra. You may sense an activation and shift in your brow as an energetic rewiring takes place. New pathways form and energies rebalance to allow function of Core Essence at the brow. Just patiently hold the space until the process seems to stabilize.

Begin slowly raising your hands again, this time to the top middle of your head at your Crown Chakra. Allow Core Essence to settle in at the crown. You may again experience a sense of rewiring and adjustment as Core Essence adjusts to this new elevated location. Setting the intention that Core Essence stays above the crown, lower your hands to relax and allow your energy to come to a new equilibrium. Take notice of the elevated frequency and give your Core Essence permission to reside in this new home space.

High Frequency Shift: Client

Moving to the head of the treatment table (seated is easier), place both hands on the Crown Chakra. Focus on your own Core Essence, maintaining frequency as high as possible. Invite Metatron to come through you, spinning Metatron's cube and entering into the client's Crown Chakra, spinning clockwise. Ask Metatron to transmute and repair the Hara as much as possible at this moment.

Hold space and observe as Metatron slowly works the cube down the Hara transmuting and clearing as he goes. Allow it to go slow and let any flaws and irregularities be repaired as the cube moves down the body. You may feel the difference as it works through each chakra and potentially any fractures within the Hara. Once it has gone all the way down to the feet, it will travel to the core of the earth, reverse spin, then slowly rise back up. Metatron may oscillate his cube up and down a few times to assure that the Hara is smooth and expanded.

Next, move along the client's body to near their Throat Chakra. Bringing your awareness to the client, visualize or sense where the client's Core Essence vibration rests. Most people have the Core Essence between heart and throat. If they have done this work before or have a strong spiritual practice it may be higher. Gently invite the client's Core Essence to rise in frequency. Using your hands, encourage their Core Essence to move toward the Throat Chakra as the frequency shifts up. Partial movement is okay if it is slow to respond.

Holding your hands above the Throat Chakra, visualize lifting the Core Essence up a few inches. As it comes up, visualize a Merkaba forming above the throat, with Core Essence encapsulated in the Merkaba.

Slowly move your hands, and the Merkaba up the client's face until it rests above the Brow Chakra. Pause at that position to allow time for Core Essence to come to equilibrium at the brow. Many people sense a restructuring or rewiring that happens as the brow adapts to the higher frequency of Core Essence. When it has stabilized, again slowly move your hands to the top of the head above the Crown Chakra. Hold that position for a while to allow time for the crown to integrate and stabilize. You or the client may again sense rewiring or energetic shifts as Core Essence adapts to this new location. Set the intention that Core Essence can now reside above the crown at this higher frequency.

Chapter Twelve

Advanced High Frequency Shift

The Advanced High Frequency Shift (AHFS) is a higher frequency version of the Basic High Frequency Shift (BHFS) in the previous chapter. We think that it would be wise to practice and integrate the BHFS before attempting to work with the advanced version. When the AHFS was introduced in our workshop, we only allowed students that had become familiar with the BHFS to attend. Then we added the upgrades step by step as they learned and experienced modules that entrained that upgraded energy into their energy bodies.

Similarly, we recommend working with and experiencing the energy of each of the previous sections before upgrading to the AHFS. This is an essential part of the work and a recommended daily practice. We believe it is one of the important keys to accessing the highest frequencies now available on the planet.

This Advanced High Frequency Shift (AHFS) has more elements and will seem more complicated, however it is a much higher frequency and opens new doorways. With practice, it becomes second nature and can be done quickly. When proficient, one can sequence through the steps in just a few moments. As noted previously, when we voice-guide meditations, we typically spend several minutes. When learning, going slowly through it allows one to fully experience and integrate the depth of energetic shifts at each step of the process. One may also realize that the more they practice, the deeper they go.

Invocation/Intention

The first step is to invoke our spiritual guides. Include your personal guides as well as the angelic helpers. We invite in different spiritual helpers depending on the type of work we are doing. We almost always invoke archangels Michael, Gabriel, Raphael, Uriel, Metatron, and Raziel. In addition to these six, many others will be situationally called upon. It is also important to set the intentionality of the work you are doing, whether you are doing a healing session or just your daily energy hygiene. The first level of intention we always set is that all will be to the highest good. This overarching intention is important, and it also inherently acknowledges that our conscious minds cannot begin to comprehend what that possibly means. Our limited understanding of "highest good" needs to be put aside to allow for the unfolding of a much grander plan. We may also have some secondary intentions for our session, such as healing emotional or physical pain.

Protection

The protection step focuses on creating sacred space within and around us for our work. The first step is to envision yourself connected to the Divine Source. How we do that can be very individual as we all have different notions of what Divine Source means. This needs to be your personal connection to "God," the universe, or some higher power. One simple way to visualize that is having a power cord connecting us to the Divine. Just plug in that cord!

Once connected to Source, we visualize a coating of pure white light that flows over and surrounds us, covering like paint. If working with a client, cover them with the same protective layers as well. Follow the white layer with a coating of iridescent rainbow colors. Cover that layer with a coating of gold glitter, sparkling all over you. We then bring in an element of sacred geometry. Visualize that you are surrounded in a protective bubble. The bubble has the geometry of the flower of life and shimmers with iridescent rainbow colors. We hold this protection in place as we work with the energy system of ourselves and our clients.

Hara Attunement and Anchoring

Attuning, anchoring or setting the Hara activates that vertical line of energy that exists in the dimension of intentionality and focuses our connection to earth and purpose in life. We begin by tuning into the energy of the planet. We connect with a transmuted earth that is the emerging future. This version of the planet has the higher frequencies that align with our evolving human consciousness and our energetic ascension. It is also important that the core crystal we use to connect to within the earth is upgraded and polished, allowing the crystal to resonate with and hold the higher frequencies.

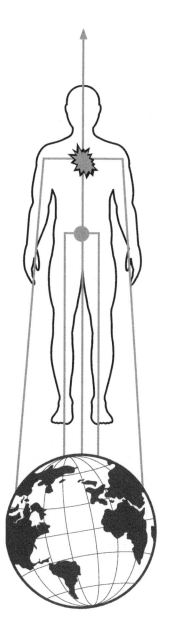

We begin by putting our awareness at our Tan Tien, in the lower abdomen. From the Tan Tien, visualize a line of energy connecting down to the very center of our planet. Anchor that line of energy from the Tan Tien to your upgraded core crystal. Consciously connect and merge your core crystal into the crystalline matrix of the earth's core. Visualize your core crystal aligning with the grid structure of the earth. Allow the frequency of Divine earth energy to flow up your connection, filling your Tan Tien.

Bring your attention to the Soul Seat, located just above the heart, and draw that earth energy into the Soul Seat. Next, focus on a point above your head, allowing the earth energy to flow straight up through the top of your head and connect to the Divine energy of the Universal Source. Pause a moment to sense the connection to Divine energy below and above. Visualize a column of light running vertically through you.

Optionally, you may focus on expanding and strengthening the Hara connection. Expand by connecting the energy from the Tan Tien out to your hips, then down your legs, connecting deep into the earth. Sense your Hara column of light grow as wide as your hips. Next focus on the Soul Seat, sending the Hara energy out to your shoulder joints and down your arms, connecting deep into the earth. Pause to sense the feeling of a stronger, wider Hara connected now by five lines to the core of the earth and the universe above.

Vivaxis Transmuting/Healing

Bring your attention to Vivaxis. Think of a hose-like connection from your left foot, off to a place in the earth somewhere near where you were born. Imagine a small sphere of light in the earth where it anchors. Sense the quality of that connection and the flow of energy. Ask your guides to transmute anything that distorts or blocks the flow of energy in your Vivaxis. Imagine it filled with swirling iridescent colors of the rainbow or the colors that allow it to flow most freely. When that connection feels clear and flowing, visualize those colors flowing up your leg, dispersing into a vapor as they rise up your thigh.

Allow that flow of colors to swirl up across the left hip, through the torso on the front side, crossing the heart and up toward your right shoulder. The colors swirl around your head, then down the back side, again crossing the heart and exiting through the entire right side of your body, connecting back to the earth. This process may be slower the first few times you do it. With regular practice you will find your Vivaxis is normally pretty clear and it goes quickly.

You may now sense an interaction between Vivaxis and 10th Chakra. Allow them to resonate and release anything in the 10th that does not serve your highest good.

Chakra Opening/Unification

The chakra opening and unification step focuses our attention on each of our chakras, sequentially. This focus opens and clears the chakra, raising its frequency as it opens. As the chakra opens it expands and flows into the Hara, unifying and blending colors into the structure of the Hara. We use the iridescent form of the colors traditionally associated with each chakra. In the Advanced High Frequency Shift (AFHS) we expand to the 12-chakra system.

Starting at Root Chakra, imagine a ball of iridescent redlight flowing into the chakra, spinning clockwise. Allow it to fill and energize the chakra, spinning faster as it opens and clears, fusing into the Hara structure. Allow time to deeply sense the chakra open, expand, and unify as the vivid red becomes one with the Hara. Set the intention it will stay spinning at that higher frequency, unified with Hara.

Bring your attention to the Sacral Chakra as you visualize an iridescent orange ball of light filling the chakra, flowing and spinning clockwise. Allow the orange light to open, expand, and fuse the sacral into the Hara. When the Sacral Chakra feels fully expanded and unified, keep it spinning and bring your attention to the Solar Plexus Chakra.

See an iridescent yellow ball of light enveloping your Solar Plexus Chakra, flowing and spinning clockwise. Allow the yellow light to open, expand, and fuse the solar plexus into the Hara. When the Solar Plexus Chakra feels fully expanded and unified, keep it spinning and bring your attention to the Heart Chakra.

Imagine an iridescent green ball of light enveloping your Heart Chakra, flowing and spinning clockwise. Allow the green light to open, expand, and fuse the Heart Chakra into the Hara. When the Heart Chakra feels fully expanded and unified, keep it spinning and bring your attention to your Throat Chakra.

Visualize an iridescent sky-blue ball of light enveloping your Throat Chakra, flowing and spinning clockwise. Allow the blue light to open, expand, and fuse the Throat Chakra into the Hara. When your Throat Chakra feels fully expanded and unified, keep it spinning and bring your attention to the Brow Chakra.

See an iridescent indigo ball of light enveloping your Brow Chakra, flowing and spinning clockwise. Allow the indigo light to open, expand, and fuse the Brow Chakra into the Hara. When the Brow Chakra feels fully expanded and unified, keep it spinning and bring your attention to the Crown Chakra.

Imagine an iridescent violet light enveloping your Crown Chakra, flowing and spinning clockwise. Allow the violet light to open, expand, and fuse the Crown Chakra into the Hara. When your Crown Chakra feels fully expanded and unified, keep it spinning and notice how all seven chakras are spinning—with their brilliant iridescent colors flowing into Hara—and your energy frequency feels elevated.

Continue the chakra opening and unification with the 8th Chakra. Visualize iridescent silver light flowing into your 8th Chakra. Sense this chakra open, expand, and fuse into the Hara. Spin the disk of 8th Chakra at a higher frequency.

Bring your attention to 9th Chakra as you visualize iridescent copper colors swirling into the chakra. As it spins faster, it expands, opens, and unifies with the Hara, spreading the copper colors through the Hara.

Move your attention below your feet and imagine an iridescent earth tone ball of energy flowing into the 10th Chakra, spinning clockwise. It expands, opens, and unifies with the Hara, spreading the iridescent earth tones through the Hara.

Shift your attention to the 11th Chakra and visualize iridescent, metallic blue colors flowing into your hands, feet, and fascia. Feel the frequency of the 11th Chakra raising and fusing with Hara.

Finally, bring your attention to the 12th Chakra as you visualize iridescent golden colors swirling into the outer edges of your energy body, activating, and raising your frequency. Now, bring your attention to the unification of the energy of the Hara with all the chakra colors and energies.

Hara Transmuting/Repair

We believe that Hara repair is best done by our angelic guides, and Metatron is our "go-to" guide for this exercise. Metatron uses the tool of his sacred geometric shape, Metatron's cube (previously described), to recondition our Hara from the inside-out. For this step, ask for Metatron's help.

In this advanced HFS, Metatron uses a double cube. A larger version of the cube will descend through the inside of the Hara, rotating as it goes. A smaller version of the cube is connected to the larger cube. As the large cube rotates inside the Hara, the smaller cube rotates as it transverses the outer wall of the Hara. This combination of cubes repairs, renews, and transmutes the inner and outer wall of the Hara as well as all internal structures.

We ask that Metatron transmute and repair the Hara to the best condition possible today. As he does the Hara work, you may experience different sensations as your energy shifts. Sometimes it seems that his cubes stay in one place for a long time. This is usually in areas where the energy is not flowing well and much repair work is needed.

Envision Metatron inserting his spinning cubes into your Hara above the head, with the cubes spinning clockwise. As the cubes slowly descend, you may sense that they move faster or slower depending on the amount of repair work needed. The double cube slowly works down the Hara column, out below the feet and down to the core of the earth to the crystal where you anchor. There it reverses direction, spinning counterclockwise and oscillating up the Hara until passing above your head. The cubes then reverse direction again and make a second pass slowly descending, spinning clockwise. The second pass is usually a little quicker as most of the work is done on the first pass. Occasionally, a third pass will be needed.

After Metatron has completed the work, invite Archangel Raziel to fill your Hara with a tapestry of golden and iridescent rainbow light, infusing your Hara with the highest frequencies you can hold.

Now that the inner work is complete with the Hara, the Magenta Warriors come in at the base of the Hara. Swirling clockwise with an iridescent magenta energy, they spiral up the outside walls of the Hara polishing and cleaning. When they reach the top of the Hara a Divine anointing oil flows down coating the outer walls of the Hara which creates protection and sealing of the outer structure.

Pause and sense your renewed and brilliant Hara.

Core Essence & Hara Expansion

The following description is a slower and deeper version of Core Essence expansion. We recommend that you periodically use this slow version as it allows for deeper clearing and heightened sensitivity to the amount of "stuff" we carry in our energy field. We do not need to carry that unnecessary baggage, and we can learn to travel lighter through our daily lives. In our recommended daily practice, you can move through the expansion in a few breaths.

Bring your hands over your heart space. Sense deep within your core being, connecting with your Core Essence. Imagine your Core Essence as a brilliant blue-white star deep in your body. Acknowledge that Divine spark that is your true self. As you focus on your Core

Essence, visualize your star getting brighter and expanding into every cell of your physical body. Feel it light up your entire being.

Using your breath, as you breathe out, continue to slowly expand your Core Essence beyond the boundary of your skin, out into the first layer of your energetic body. Light up and clear your etheric body layer. Expand your Hara so it, too, fills the space of the etheric body.

As you breathe in, imagine your Core Essence drawing back to a point of light deep within. On your next exhalation, slowly expand your Core Essence out into the second layer, your emotional energetic body. Sense it light up and clear your emotional body. Let Core Essence dissolve all the emotional energy that you are holding in this body. Pause here for a breath or two, if needed, to fully clear this layer. Be aware of the calmness that comes. Then expand your Hara so that it now extends out to the edge of your emotional body.

Again as you breathe in, imagine your Core Essence drawing back to a point of light deep within. Exhale and slowly expand your Core Essence out into the third layer, your mental energetic body. Sense it light up and clear your mental body. Let Core Essence dissipate all the thought forms and mental energy that you are holding in this body. Pause here for a breath to fully clear this layer and sense the clarity of a revitalized mental body. Then expand your Hara so that it now extends out to the edge of the mental body.

Breathe in and draw Core Essence back to a point of light deep within. Exhale and slowly expand your Core Essence out into the fourth layer, your astral energetic body. Sense it light up, clear, and vitalize your astral body. Pause here for a breath, if needed, to fully clear and sense this layer. Then expand your Hara so that it extends out to the edge of your astral body.

Breathing in, draw Core Essence back to a point of light. Exhale, slowly expanding Core Essence out into your fifth layer, the etheric template energetic body. This is the blueprint of your physical body. Let Core Essence light up and flow through all the lines and grids of this layer, clearing and vitalizing your etheric template. Pause here for a breath to sense the difference in this layer. Next, expand your Hara so that it extends out to the edge of the etheric template layer.

Breathe in, drawing Core Essence back to that point of light deep within. Exhaling slowly, expand your Core Essence out into the sixth layer, your celestial energetic body. Sense how iridescent colors flood and expand your celestial body. Pause here for a breath to experience your brilliance. Expand your Hara so that it fills to the edge of the celestial body.

Again, as you breathe in, Core Essence draws back to a point of light. Next exhale slowly to expand your Core Essence out, fully extending into your seventh layer, the ketheric energetic body. Expand your Hara to the edge of the Ketheric body.

Breathe in, drawing Core Essence back to a point of light. Exhaling slowly, expand your Core Essence into the field associated with the 8th Chakra. Now, expand your Hara to the 8th field.

Breathe in once more and Core Essence draws back to a point of light. On your next exhalation, slowly expand your Core Essence out, filling the field of the 9th Chakra. Expand your Hara with Core Essence to the 9th field.

Breathe in, drawing Core Essence back to a point of light. As you exhale, slowly expand your Core Essence into the field associated with the 10th Chakra. Now expand your Hara to the 10th field.

Again as you breathe in, Core Essence draws back to a point of light. Next exhale slowly and expand your Core Essence out, filling the field of your 11th Chakra. Expand your Hara with Core Essence to the 11th and Fascial Grids.

Finally, breathe in and draw Core Essence back to a point of light. As you exhale, expand your Core Essence out, filling the outer layers of your energy body and 12th Chakra. Expand your Hara with Core Essence to the outer extent of your energy bubble.

Core Essence lights up the golden bubble of energy that surrounds you. Hara fills and expands into your entire energetic being. Feel your pure full expansion and remember this feeling so you can come here often. Hold Core Essence in this expanded state.

Bring Hara back to a size that feels comfortable to you. This may change over time and be situational. Most people find that a Hara expansion of 3–4 feet feels right. If you are going out in public places most people are better served by having a more compact energy body. Only if you have practiced good clear boundaries, should you have a large, expanded field out in public places.

Core Essence Elevation

Elevation of our Core Essence is a key part of accessing the higher frequencies now available. This description is for a slower version which is essential when first learning and wise to use occasionally if you are able to put this in daily practice. It has been our experience that once Core Essence is elevated, it is like unlocking access to the frequencies. Core Essence will tend to stay elevated if practiced regularly. If not lovingly cared for, it will drift back to our old lower frequency.

Following expansion of Core Essence, bring your hands to your chest, holding them over your heart space. Connect into that spark of Core Essence. Simultaneously connect into your Oversoul, resonating with the highest frequency of your Soul in this plane. Visualize the connection between Core Essence and Oversoul. Let your Core Essence rise to the highest level it can reach.

Take notice of the elevated frequency and give your Core Essence permission to reside in this new home space.

Advanced High Frequency Shift: Client

The Advanced High Frequency Shift for the client is very close to the version described in the Basic High Frequency Shift section previously, with a few additions to include. The first is to include clearing of the client's Vivaxis, which was not part of the earlier description.

When working with the client's Vivaxis, first focus on the sphere where the Vivaxis is connected to the earth. Ask the guides to help. Ask that the sphere connection be shifted to connect with the new transmuted earth, which will give it a higher frequency connection. Visualize it connecting to the earth grids and crystal matrix of the planet.

Next focus on the connection between the sphere and the left foot of the client. Work with the guides to clear any blockages or distortions. They may use any range of colors or elements to clear the flow. When good flow is established, check to see that it flows through the body optimally. Again, using the guides to assist as needed.

Chapter Thirteen

Creation of the
Fall 2020 Workshop

All of our work is very heavily guided by our pantheon of guides. Sometimes it seems we are a bit slow as humans to translate the new material and bring it into a teachable format. About a week before the Fall 2020 Workshop, Tim was getting a massage. As usual, the guides were busy feeding his therapist information for him. They said something along the lines of: *"You think you have a lot to do to get ready, but you wouldn't believe all that we have to do on our end to make this happen."*

During the workshop we felt the incredible changes the guides were making shifts to the very matrix of our world to bring these wonderfully transformative energies into the planet. We realize that this work is merely one part of the many efforts the unseen world is making to help humanity awaken and move into a new way of being.

Our workshop creation had been falling into a familiar pattern after experiencing the first couple workshops. Our focus was usually just on the upcoming workshop. Occasionally we would get guided information that seemed to fit in a future workshop. When that happened, we put it aside and focused on the task at hand. We would tell our guides to just wait and do one thing at a time. As soon as we completed a workshop and the participants went home, information for the next workshop would start flowing in. As the content of each workshop is primarily new material, this process seemed to work.

The year of 2020 was a bit different due to the chaos of Covid19. We were planning a spring workshop and had all the material ready when we canceled due to the pandemic and a need to avoid large gatherings.

Our 3D brains thought that this would make the fall workshop preparation easy as we would just use the spring curriculum in the fall. Our guides had a different idea. We were able to reuse small portions of our spring preparations; however, most of the workshop became new material, as usual.

The new material related to the Lightbody came in with virus-related concerns. In the spring of 2020, as Covid19 spread, numerous discussion threads on the internet were focusing on blaming the roll-out of 5G cell technology as the reason for the spread of the human virus. Checking with our guidance and the science, we were informed that 5G does play some role, however the primary 5G impact is on the Lightbody rather than the physical body.

Disturbances to the Lightbody ultimately translate into the physical. Given the vast investments in this technology and the limits and speed of science to demonstrate a link, we thought it would be unlikely that 5G would be stopped in the near future. Our queries then related to ways to protect oneself. We were given two ways to assist:

- One way related to frequency. If the 5G interferes within a certain frequency range, then if the Lightbody frequency moved to a different frequency, the interferences would be reduced. We also started getting information about DNA modifications. It seemed that changes in Lightbody would potentially also affect our DNA.

- The second way is to provide energetic protection shielding in an analog to the physical protection of a faraday EMF shield.

The first idea came through during a triad guidance discussion. The second idea came as the guides helped during a client healing session. Both these ideas ended up being woven into the treatment protocols of the retreat.

Around the time our spring retreat was canceled, we started to receive information about the Rays. It was coming to us in client treatments, triad discussions, and as another in the AHA community sent us a book. We continued to get more information about Rays and Lightbody. They were showing us in client work that Lightbody can be infected with energetic parasites and damaged in various ways. We spent weeks in the summer meditating and focusing on the

Rays, one each day until we had experienced each of them a few times. We also were starting to get more nudges about Primary Cell.

We had incorporated that concept a few workshops back, but it was coming to us in a renewed version, begging for incorporation in the work. Around midsummer a client session brought in the concept of integrating and unifying the Hara and chakra systems. We continued to experiment, work, and refine that idea over the summer as we worked on self and with clients. We found this work had a profound effect on our High Heart and Soul connections. The Oversoul concept started appearing as we felt we were moving Core Essence to an ever-higher frequency. We also sensed our triad was connecting more at an Oversoul level as our energies continued to evolve. We were finding that all aspects of our energetic system were changing as we worked with the Lightbody and the Chakra/Hara Unification.

By late summer DNA kept coming up in the work and it seemed to be woven with some of the ideas of neural plasticity that we were hoping to weave in. Throughout the summer we kept getting more information regarding the upper chakras (8–12). We were led to shift all the materials into a consistent 12-chakra system rather than a mix of 7 and 12 chakras. By September, this workshop was mostly coming together, but a few pieces just seemed to be elusive. Another group of dimensional beings showed up around that time. The group we call the Comet Beings. They work in the space between all matter and extra-dimensionally. Their frequency was a good fit for some of the protocols.

One of the few pieces of the spring material we used was related to a group of guides we affectionately call the Star Beings. When we finished our fall 2019 retreat, we came back to the house we had rented for our preparation and debrief times. Jeannette had been brought in "virtually" for the retreat but was able to physically join us a day later for a post-retreat debrief.

As we worked and waited for Jeannette to arrive, we noticed a group of beings just hanging around (invisibly) in the backyard. They, too, seemed to be just waiting and not wanting to communicate. Once we were all assembled and joined in meditation, the Star Beings made themselves available and began communicating with us. We had been planning protocols using the geometry of C^{60} atoms, also known as fullerenes. They used that geometric pattern to create a vehicle bringing us all to a vision of their star space. During this vision we were introduced to the frequency of a new material that they would show us how to use in our work. They joined our guides during the next workshop as we used this new material frequency in the protocols.

Chapter Fourteen

Opening Invocation: October 2020

We began the workshop in ceremony, using the following invocation to set the frequency and intention for the following days. The ceremony included a ritual to join as a group and move into multidimensional awareness.

Amplifying Higher Frequencies: Greater Alignment with Divine Consciousness

I step onto the new earth, fusing with the fluid crystalline matrix as my awareness expands.

I connect here with the earth grids and the minerals, experiencing a deep connection to all elements and the wisdom of Mother Earth.

I honor the ancestors and elemental beings protecting this space.

I invoke the light of the earth, stars, and moon to move into and through me, transmuting me into a pure vessel.

I breathe in, opening and embracing new frequencies as the Rays of Light move through me.

I stand as a beacon of unification welcoming new awareness of the Divine Holographic Lightbody that I am.

I open my heart and mind as a child, embracing the alchemy of full DNA in resonance with the Divine light, letting it fill me, and transform me.

Workshop Experientials

The experiential portion of the workshop is where the amazing energy of high frequency does its work. Through these experiences, the participants have the opportunity to both give and receive the work. All of the following exercises are done as an energy healing trade. Participants pair up. One assumes the role of the practitioner, while the other takes on the role of the client or recipient of the work. We refer to the person receiving as a client. When on the table receiving the work, powerful healing experiences can happen. Often, people have reported profound life changing shifts. The practitioner may also have profound experiences as witness to the multidimensional healing energy flow. After the session is complete and time is taken for discussion and reflection, the participants reverse roles so that both have an opportunity to give and receive.

This exchange anchors in the frequencies and allows the participants to remember and reproduce the sessions after the workshop. Some participants have healing practices and will replicate the work with their clients, spreading the frequencies and healing. Others may be participating primarily for self healing. Self-care versions of the experiences are provided for all participants, allowing them to continue their healing self-care at home.

Our intention is set for the recipient's highest good at this time in their life journey. This is guided work. We ask for the highest frequency level of guidance needed that will help the recipient today. These sequences have a number of steps, so it is best to have this printed material in front of you to help when first practicing, until the practitioner can do it from memory.

Chapter Fifteen

Importance of Boundaries

In this workshop, boundaries took a new twist. We were asked to bring forward the relationship between all the grids and fields, looking at boundaries from a multidimensional perspective.

When we continue to do our self-work to be the clearest vessel for personal evolution as well as being the space for a client, and continue to work from a higher frequency, lower frequencies within the body and energy system get cleared. Thus we are less likely to get triggered when another transgresses our boundaries. The key is to do one's own personal work to clear congested, stuck, or traumatic lower frequencies that hinder us from holding a high frequency.

This is a daily practice that we each strive to hold a greater amount of light within our physical being and energy being. Working with personal boundaries from a place of high frequency shifts us out of a me/them place and elevates us to a place of the Soul level and working with collective consciousness.

We are all in this together and our goal is to be deeply present and loving for self and others. A Heart-centered way of being, as well as self-compassion and presence with self and others from this place, can transmute lower frequencies that keep us from having healthy personal and collective boundaries.

Chapter Sixteen

Working in the Realms of Plasma

When doing energy work it is quite tempting to focus on the physical reality. Most often our clients' complaints are physical in nature, and most of our daily focus is in the 3D reality of the physical. We find that most of the time, physical manifestations of disease and pain are rooted in nonphysical phenomena. When working with the energy centers and energy fields it becomes apparent that much of what needs to change is not in the physical. So, in reality much of energy work can happen in the space between spaces rather than focusing entirely on the physical. Using the notion of plasma allows for greater creative visualization to work in the non-physical rather than the physical.

To introduce the idea of plasma we bring participants on a visual journey in order to understand the vastness of the large-scale world of our galaxy and beyond. Similarly, there is also a vastness in the smallest dimensions of the physical. In the scientific view, plasma is one of the four fundamental states of matter. It consists of a gas of ions which have had some of their electrons stripped off. That makes it highly conductive. Space is filled with plasma in ways that we are only beginning to understand. The vastness of space is not truly an empty vacuum as we once thought. There are sheets and flows of plasma that occupy this space. It may turn out that plasma is actually the most abundant form of mass in the universe. Our definition of plasma includes this scientific view, but also encompasses the unseen energies that also follow through the universe. There is a term in older writing called "ether" for the stuff that fills the voids of space. Scientific views obsoleted that use of the word. Perhaps the original use of that word had more validity than we give credit.

After taking a tour of the vastness of large-scale, we take participants on a tour of nanoscale and smaller. When we look at the dimensions of matter, the scales of small are similar to the scales of large. For instance, the nucleus of a typical atom and its surrounding electrons has a scale that is similar to our solar system in miniature. So, an atom is thought to be mostly empty space much like our solar system. Matter at all scales is primarily composed of empty spaces. We think that there is a plasma-like energy that flows through all those empty spaces or voids in both the large and small scales.

When working with energy, it is useful to understand the "void" nature of matter and allow the energies we use to flow through those voids into all things. Rather than visualize energy flowing into the more solid notion of the matter we tend to see, we expand to visualize energy working in between and through all matter.

It is on this scale that our friends—the Comet Beings—come in to help. When we can visualize working in the plasma level with energy, we can tap into the Comet Beings. As the energy flows, these little multidimensional beings zip around clearing and shifting things on the smallest of scales, interconnecting through the many dimensions of our existence.

Chapter Seventeen

Experiencing the
12 Rays of Light

A "Ray of Light" is a title given to a specific or focused aspect of the consciousness of our Creator. The consciousness of the Creator pervades the entire universe. The various Rays of Light are different frequencies of the same one light, the energy of pure Divine love that subtly guides and informs our reality. Our work draws on the teachings of Alice Bailey and Natalie Sian Glasson, as well our own guidance. Bailey's early writing focused on seven Rays of Light, whereas Glasson's writing covers twelve Rays. We suggest reading those resources to get a better grasp on the ideas of spiritual hierarchies and the many teachers that are available to us as we work with the Rays of Light. Even without that more detailed understanding of the hierarchy, we can ask for the guidance of those world teachers and masters to assist in our work and our personal growth. One only needs to ask for their assistance and they are ready and willing to help.

Prior to including this material in our workshop, we spent time in meditation with each of the Rays to experience them and allow them to work on us. Initially we adopted a "Ray a day" program where we would read about one Ray and spend time in meditation with that Ray. Throughout the day, we would come back to feel and experience the Ray. At night, we would ask to be taken to the ashram or spiritual school associated with that Ray. The next day, we would spend time with another Ray. We did that for 24 days, experiencing each Ray and the guardians twice. We then moved into a more random experience by asking our guides which Rays to work with and then working with two or three Rays at once as a way to integrate ourselves with the frequency of the Rays.

What follows are the highlights of each Ray and associated master for each Ray. As you read about each Ray, pause, and spend a few quiet moments with that Ray. Ask the master of the Ray and the helpers to bring the frequency of that Ray into your body and experience the frequency deep within.

The first three Rays are primary Rays.

1st Ray – Red: Master for this Ray is El Morya (known as the biblical Abraham in an earthly incarnation).

This Ray comes in the crown flowing down through the body, bringing qualities of Divine will and Divine plans. The purpose is about acting and existing per the will of our Creator. Angelic helpers associated with this Ray include Archangel Michael and Archangel Faith. The elemental kingdom can also be of assistance with this Ray.

2nd Ray – Blue: Master for this Ray is Master Joshua (known as Dr. Joshua David Stone in a recent earthly incarnation).

This Ray comes in the crown, entering the chakra and Hara column flowing down into the earth, bringing the qualities of Christ Consciousness and Divine love. Allowing this blue energy of love to merge with your physical, energetic, and all other aspects of your being. The purpose is about being, embodying, and existing as pure unconditional love. Angelic helpers associated with this Ray include Archangel Jophiel and Archangel Christine.

3rd Ray – Yellow: Master for this Ray is Master Serapis Bey (earthly incarnations in Atlantis and ancient Egypt).

This Ray comes in the crown, flowing through the body and down into the earth. It brings in the qualities of active intelligence and clarity. It illuminates the mind and aids in manifestations of mental constructs. The purpose is about mastery of the mind and understanding our energetic self. Angelic helpers associated with this Ray include Archangel Chamuel and Archangel Charity.

The fourth through seventh Rays are aspects of the 3rd Ray.

4th Ray – Green: Master for this Ray is Paul the Venetian (most known earthly incarnation as Michelangelo).

This Ray comes in and integrates into our physical being and Soul. It brings in the qualities of harmony, beauty, creativity, arts, music, drama, and dance. The purpose of this Ray is about the expression of our Creator. Angelic helpers associated with this Ray include Archangel Gabriel and Archangel Hope.

5th Ray – Orange: Master for this Ray is Master Hilarion (known as the apostle Paul and philosopher Lamblichus in earthly incarnations).

This Ray comes in through a higher dimensional space. It brings in the qualities of Divine expression of the Creators' mind. It energizes science, ideas, and tools. The purpose of this Ray is discovery, Soul acceptance, and alignment with our Creator. Angelic helpers associated with this Ray include Archangel Raphael and Archangel Mary.

6th Ray – Indigo: Master for this Ray is Master Lanto (Chinese Master and disciple of Christ in earthly incarnations).

This Ray comes in bathing us in love and devotion. It brings in the qualities of a deep devotion of the Divine. The purpose is about total surrender to the love and devotion of our Creator. Angelic helpers associated with this Ray include Archangel Uriel and Archangel Aurora.

7th Ray – Violet: Master for this Ray is Lady Portia (a feminine aspect of St. Germaine, with incarnations on Earth and Venus).

This Ray comes in when we invoke violet flames to engulf and purify ourselves. It brings in qualities of accelerated awareness, loving, and spiritual transformation. The purpose is about consciousness and acceptance of truth. Angelic helpers associated with this Ray include Archangel Zadkiel and Archangel Amethyst.

The Rays eight through twelve come from higher in the hierarchy at the level of planetary logos.

8th Ray – Seafoam green or a soft mint color: Master for this Ray is Lady Nada (feminine aspect of Jesus, with incarnations on Venus).

This Ray comes into and over our bodies. It brings in the qualities of purity, cleanliness, and at—one—ment with the Creator. The purpose is cleansing our Soul and spiritual layers. Angelic helpers associated with this Ray include Archangel Jeremiel and Archangel Josephine. The Pleiadeans also support this Ray.

9th Ray – Blue green, as green grass below a blue sky: Master for this Ray is Lady Mary (incarnations as mother of Jesus and Horus).

This Ray comes in the crown flowing down through the body into the earth. It brings in the qualities of Soul understanding, Soul growth, and anchoring in the planetary Lightbody. The purpose is about Soul exploration and pure joy. Lady Mary coordinates with the 5th Ray working closely with Archangel Raphael and Archangel Mary. The Sirians also support this Ray.

10th Ray – Pearlescent: Masters for this Ray are Lady Andromeda (Vessa – the energy of goddess) and Master Andromeda.

This Ray comes in and surrounds us in a pearlescent cocoon. It brings in the qualities of Soul acceptance and Soul merge at the planetary level. The purpose is about Soul integration. The Andromedans are the helpers of this Ray.

11th Ray – Peach, a blend of pink and orange: Master for this Ray is Lady Quan Yin (Divine Mother).

As this Ray comes in, it feels as if you are held in the loving arms of the Divine Mother. It brings in the qualities of anchoring the pure Divine love of manifestation and reinforces and brings the embodiment of all the other Rays. The purpose is about resting and integration of all lessons. It is about deeper Soul integration and the merging of the Soul aspects of the monad. Associated helpers are the Great White Brotherhood/Sisterhood of Ascended Masters.

12th Ray – Golden: Master for this Ray is Pallas Athena (Greek goddess and warrior).

As this Ray comes in, it integrates the pure love of Christ Consciousness into your being. It brings in the qualities of Christ light directly from the Creator Soul at a planetary level. The purpose is about complete Soul integration with Christ Consciousness. Associated helpers are Lord Maitreya, Lord Melchizedek, and Archangel Metatron.

Workshop Experiential

We created this experiential healing exercise to provide the participants with an opportunity to deeply invite the frequencies to work,
heal, and open new pathways. This exercise is done as an energy
healing trade. Participants pair up. One assumes the role of the
practitioner, the other the role of client or recipient of the work.
After the session is complete and time is taken for discussion
and reflection, the participants reverse roles so that both have
an opportunity to give and receive.

The purpose of this technique is to:

- Awaken the highest frequencies of the Rays of Light within the
  physical, emotional, mental, and spiritual bodies.
- Purify the multidimensional levels of self to facilitate releasing
  of lower frequencies. (trauma, distortions, congested energies,
  negative thoughtforms, etc.)
- Embodying connection to the Rays of Light that facilitate Soul
  development at this time.
- Assist in the collective Soul development.
- Support anchoring the Rays into Mother Earth.

High Frequency Shift: Self

The first step of the session is Advanced High Frequency Shift (AHFS)
for the practitioner. This is done while holding the feet of the client.
The AHFS brings the practitioner to the optimum elevated frequency
to be the conduit for the client. It also serves to entrain the client in that
elevated frequency, beginning the process of healing.

High Frequency Shift: Client

The next step is to perform the client version of the AHFS, assuring
the client is also at an elevated frequency.

Infusion of the Rays

The unique part of the protocol begins with the practitioner holding
the client's feet. The practitioner invites in the energy of the plasma,

supported by the Comet Beings. The energy swirls up the client's physical being, embodying the consciousness of the Creator. This opens and prepares the client's energy system to receive the Rays.

Next the practitioner moves alongside the client, placing one hand on the Heart Chakra, the other hand on the High Heart (thymus). Normally, this is done with hands on the body but is equally effective if hands are above the body. Prior to starting, the practitioner and client have discussed the Rays and intuitively chosen three Rays to experience in this session. Three are chosen for practicality. It would take considerably longer to experience all twelve in one session and may be more than the client's system can effectively integrate.

The practitioner invites in the frequency of the first Ray chosen to be experienced. The practitioner then holds space and becomes the receiving vessel to allow that Ray to infuse, fill, and radiate through the client. Clients are advised to simply stay in a receptive mode, aware and observant of the sensations, thoughts, images, and experiences. This position is held for some time until the energy flow subsides and the practitioner senses completion. We have allowed about five minutes for the first chosen Ray in this process. It could be shorter or much longer depending on the client and situation. The same process is used to allow the client to experience one or two more Rays.

Following completion of the Ray infusion, the practitioner steps back and stretches out their arms. The intention is to hold the edge of the client's aura (Ketheric body). Holding the edge of the aura, the practitioner focuses on unification and integration of the experienced Rays with the client's Soul. That position is held until the integration feels complete.

Next step is "zipping up the field". This is done starting with holding the palms of both hands on the soles of the feet. The practitioner holds each position for about 15–20 seconds, allowing the energy to flow, with the intention of sealing in the work. Work your way up the body "zipping" in the sequence listed on the next page.

1. Hands on bottom of feet.
2. Left ankle and right knee.
3. Right ankle and left knee.
4. Left knee and right hip.
5. Right knee and left hip.
6. Both hips.
7. Left wrist and right elbow.
8. Right wrist and left elbow.
9. Left elbow and right shoulder.
10. Right elbow and left shoulder.
11. Both shoulders.
12. Left shoulder and right side of the head.
13. Right shoulder and left side of the head.
14. Both sides of the head.

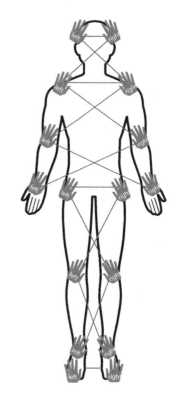

The practitioner then returns to the client's feet, visualizing rich iridescent neon orange earth energy flowing into the feet and up the body, flooding the bones, fascia, organs, and every cell of the body. The practitioner also intends this energy to flow through the Vivaxis, Hara, and all grounding connections, fully connecting the client back with the planet. This step supports the client in anchoring all manifestations of the Ray energies into physical form.

As a final step, the practitioner visualizes streamers of gossamer threads woven and infused with iridescent diamonds, swirling around, and creating a three-inch-thick cocoon of energy. This protects and holds the energy allowing time to integrate and assimilate the gifts of the session.

Chapter Eighteen

Quantum Mind Clearance

This protocol is based on the work of the late Reverend Rudy Noël, published in his book *The Huggin' Healer*. Franny assisted with his publication, and in her studies with Rudy, he shared in-depth nuances of this protocol with her. Tim and Jeannette are familiar with Healing Touch Program's adaptation of his work and have used versions of his technique for years. The earlier version we had been using was practiced at different frequencies we had attuned to as we learned it years prior. We had the idea to try his technique running the new higher frequencies that we would be using in the workshop. As soon as the "experiment" started, Rudy was in the room, delighted to be part of the session. As the work progressed, Rudy guided it back to the format of his original work. We also realized that this new higher frequency was closer to what Rudy really wanted. Although the technique uses hand positions primarily around the head, it acts in the full body, resonating through the meridians, chakras, and all fields and grids.

The purpose of this technique is to:

- Promote trust with the client. It is an excellent treatment beginning technique as it creates a safe, calm, loving space.

- Open and balance the energy system, allowing higher frequencies to transmute and dissolve denser/hidden lower frequencies.

- Balance the brain and bring a deep sense of calm to the client. Clearing the mental and emotional states and calming the nervous system.

- Connect the head and heart, moving out of "the story" into the Soul lessons.

- Transmute energy of the physical heart and move the heart energetically to align with high heart. This facilitates moving the heart from fear and guilt-driven responses to pure love-driven, Soul-oriented responses.

- Prepare the energetic system to embrace our evolution.

- Relieve stress-related headaches if present. This is helpful for concentration issues, dyslexia, epilepsy, brain tumors, and ADHD.

Per our standard recommendation, we believe that the technique works best if the preliminary steps to shift frequency are utilized prior to the steps of the Quantum Mind Clearance protocol. Typically, this technique is performed with a client horizontal on a treatment table, however, it can also be practiced on a seated client. If the client is seated, some hand positions may need to be modified to make it anatomically possible. The intentionality of the sequence will guide the work, even with the minor modifications.

High Frequency Shift: Self

The first step of the session is Advanced High Frequency Shift (AHFS) for the practitioner. This is done while holding the feet of the client. The AHFS brings the practitioner to the optimum elevated frequency to be the conduit for the client. It also serves to entrain the client in that elevated frequency, beginning the process of healing.

High Frequency Shift: Client

The next step is to perform the client version of the AHFS, assuring the client is also at an elevated frequency.

Quantum Mind Clearance

The unique part of the protocol entails twelve steps. Each of the steps is detailed below with illustrations to guide placement of the hands. Each of the hand positions uses a light touch. We often say imagine touching with the weight of a coin, at each finger placement. In each position, hold until the energy movement subsides, or it feels complete. If unsure, hold for about a minute in each position.

1. This initial hold taps into the meridian system and opens the entire chakra system of the client.

Hold the head in your cupped hands, with three or four fingers from each hand along the occipital ridge.

Attune and run feminine energy until it matches the client's energy.

Intentionally raise your frequency until the client feels energy throughout the body down to the feet. You may notice the energy moves through the client's body, activating energetic flows.

Some traction pressure may feel good. If using traction, check with the client to assure it is safe. If they have neck injuries and cervical spinal issues, do not use traction.

2. Thumbs rest on the blood pressure point at the top of the head (Crown Chakra), with fingers of the hand pointed down, capping the top back of head like a beanie.

Allow the energy to flow into the meridians and nervous system until it feels balanced.

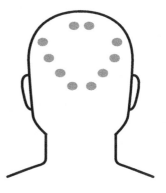

This position is known to be beneficial in reducing excessive blood pressure.

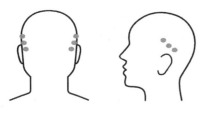

3. Brain balance: this position is very calming. Often clients will cease talking and move to a deeper quiet with this position.

Middle fingers are placed on the indentation along the ridge above the ears.

Allow undulating energy until the pulse is even in both hands. You can visualize energy moving slowly, like a ping pong ball, going back and forth between the hemispheres.

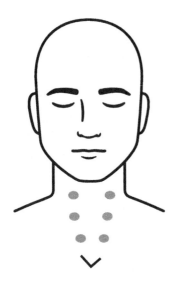

4. This position balances the thyroid and parathyroid glands.

Lightly place three fingers on each side of Adam's apple.

Allow the energy to flow into the glands until they seem filled.

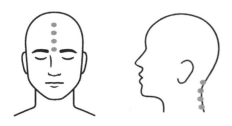

5. This position runs energy down the middle of the brain through the corpus callosum. The corpus callosum is the major communication link between brain hemispheres.

Place one hand behind the head, with fingers on the cervical spine (C-2 to C-5).

The other hand is positioned on the brow, with fingers from the ridge of the nose to the hairline.

Allow the energy to flow between hands until it feels connected and balanced.

6. This position works with the frontal lobe and the Brow Chakra.

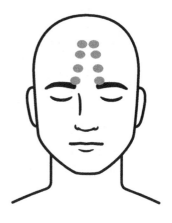

Position fingertips on the forehead.

Place three or four fingers from each hand along a line from the INSIDE of the eyebrows to the middle of the hairline.

This creates a small triangle with the Brow Chakra at the base of the triangle.

Allow the energy to flow until balanced.

7. As you move from the previous step to this step, the top fingers stay in place. The lower fingers spread the triangle, opening at the Brow Chakra.

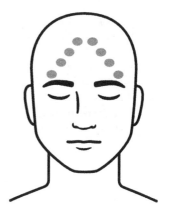

It ends with a wider triangle, three or four fingers from each hand along a line OUTSIDE the eyebrows to the middle of the hairline.

Again, allow the energy to flow until balanced.

8. This loving nurturing gesture lightly traces the shape of a heart three times across the face.

Each heart shape starts with both thumbs, transitioning to palms of hand as you sweep down the cheeks.

1st heart: From the bridge of the nose to across the eyebrows and down the cheeks, creating a heart shape.

2nd heart: From the bridge of the nose to across the mid-brow and down the cheeks, enlarging the heart shape.

3rd heart: From the bridge of the nose to the top of the hairline and down the cheeks, creating a larger heart shape.

9. Follow the sweeping of the previous step with a loving nurturing hold.

Cup both hands lightly around the chin so that the fingers point toward the thyroid.

Gently hold and fill with the energy of pure unconditional love.

10. This position serves to connect the head and heart. We usually notice an amazing flow of energy as the head connects and communicates more effectively with the heart. It also integrates the trauma center in the right temporal lobe with the high heart.

Place the left arm so that the hand is to the left of the Heart Chakra (respectfully placed above breasts) and the client's head is resting on your forearm, as if cradling a child.

The right hand cups the right side of the skull as the thumb points toward the Crown Chakra.

Allow an undulating flow of energy between the hands.

This position beneficially addresses the pineal, pituitary, and hypothalamus glands.

11. This position facilitates integration of the physical heart connections with the Soul level aspirations of the high heart.

Place both hands over the Heart Chakra (again, respectfully above breasts).

Staying with the energy until the treatment feels complete.

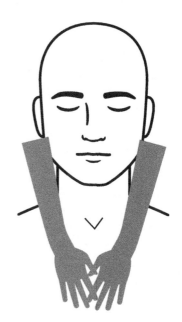

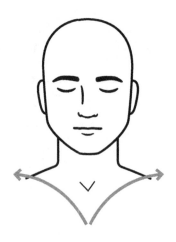

12. This step completes the treatment protocol.

Brush from the Heart Chakra to the shoulders on both sides, smoothing out the energy. Move softly so as not to startle the client.

Chapter Nineteen

Chakra/Hara Unification

This protocol first came to us when Jeannette was working with a client with blood cancer and experiencing many issues revolving around self-worth and self-love. As she was working with each chakra, spinning and clearing them, the guides had the chakra energy get drawn out front and back and fuse into the Hara. The chakra frequencies and colors became blended and unified with the Hara. This happened with each of the chakras. As the client's chakras and Hara unified, the process seemed to clear a lot of the client's old challenges.

The next morning, the client reported feeling like a new person with new vitality and a desire to go hiking. These changes continued to hold for her. As usual, the three of us all began by experimenting with this change on ourselves, as well as with clients. We quickly realized that it supported the other work that was emerging with Lightbody transformations. We also felt that this unification allowed or required an expansion of the Hara to hold these unified higher frequencies. While we had been working with the idea of bringing in Hara expansion to the workshops, this seemed to bring that need to the forefront. The protocol below comes from that guidance and refinement in practice.

The purpose of this technique is to:

- Transmute and dissolve denser/hidden lower frequencies.
- Expand and integrate the Chakras with the Hara at a higher frequency (front/back/center point).

- Erase the individuation (yet maintain individual identity) of each chakra and merge/unify back into one.
- Allow chakras to become one with the Hara within the Haric frequencies.
- Embrace the next stage of our energy body evolution.

High Frequency Shift: Self

The first step of the session is Advanced High Frequency Shift (AHFS) for the practitioner. This is done while holding the feet of the client. The AHFS brings the practitioner to the optimum elevated frequency to be the conduit for the client. It also serves to entrain the client in that elevated frequency, beginning the process of healing.

High Frequency Shift: Client

The next step is to perform the client version of the AHFS, assuring the client is also at an elevated frequency.

Clearing the Outer Grid

The unique part of the protocol begins with clearing the outer four grids of the client. As explained previously, this work is done by the guides. The practitioner goes through the motions, which act to focus the intentionality and aid the work of the guides. For each pass through the grids, the practitioner visualizes passing a large hoop down the table, imagining the hoop passing on all sides of the client. The guides create special filters for the hoop for each pass. The filter is specific to the person and the particular grid being worked on by the guides.

1st grid is the Incarnation. This grid holds information related to our current incarnation assignments. Changes to this grid may clarify alignment with the client's life purpose. Aided by our guides, we make three passes of the filters through the Incarnation Grid.

2nd grid is the Soul Field Grid. First we ask the guides to help retrieve any aspects of the Soul the client may have given away. Then we ask the client to release any aspect of the Soul of others that they might be holding. It is best to ask the client out loud to release. This step alone often has a profound effect on people. As before, aided by the guides, we make three passes of the filters through the Soul Field Grid.

3rd grid is the Fascial Grid. The Fascial Grid is instrumental in multidimensional communication between the energy fields and the physical. Shifts in this grid enhance alignment and communication. As before, aided by the guides, we make three passes of the filters through the Fascia Grid.

4th grid is the DNA Grid. This grid carries familial and genetic structures. Shifts to this grid may allow old patterns to heal backward and forward in time. Again, we make three passes of the filters through the DNA Grid.

Rainbow Light Infusion

This step brings in a frequency of rainbow light. This energy frequency is distinctly different from the frequency experienced when working with the 12 Rays. It runs at a frequency more aligned with the highest frequencies of chakra energy. The practitioner moves to the foot of the table and holds the bottom of the client's feet.

While holding the bottom of the client's feet, attune with your Core Essence as high as possible, with the Hara anchored deep into the earth. Shift to a mode of allowing, and invite the iridescent rainbow frequency to flow through the client's physical body. Allow it to flow through the bones, the fascia, skin, and all the tissues, purifying and transmuting. This step may take a few minutes or more to feel complete. Stay present and allow this movement to expand and open the energy fields to create space for the frequencies to flow freely.

Chakra/Hara Unification

Before starting the unification process, it is best if we have a visual of the flow in our mind's eye. Standing on the right side of the client and looking toward their head (face up), imagine the energy flowing up and out of the center and rotating around the center point at each chakra. As we work with each one, we will move our hands in circles similar to the flow: Clockwise from the center would move to the practitioner's right, while counterclockwise will move to the practitioner's left.

We begin with the Root Chakra, visualizing iridescent red light in the chakra. Start rotating both hands over the Root Chakra simultaneously. Our right hand flowing from the center of the chakra toward the client's left hip, and our left hand flowing from the center of the chakra toward the right hip. Continue to rotate in each direction, with each stroke moving farther and farther out toward the edge of the client's Hara. Allow the chakra to blend, dissipate, and fully unify with the Hara. You may experience the rich iridescent red colors of the root flowing into and unifying with Hara.

Moving up to the 2nd Sacral Chakra, we repeat the process, rotating our hands in ever widening circles unifying the iridescent orange of the sacral into the Hara.

Continuing up the chakra column, we perform the same motions using the following colors:

Iridescent yellow – 3rd Solar Plexus

Iridescent emerald green – 4th Heart

Iridescent sky blue – 5th Throat

Iridescent indigo – 6th Brow

Iridescent violet – 7th Crown

Iridescent silver – 8th

Iridescent copper – 9th Soul Star

Below the feet, Iridescent earth tone – 10th Earth Star

Moving to the head, rotate both hands above the head, connecting into the 11th Chakra simultaneously, by flowing both hands from above the head through the center of the body. Continue to rotate your hands in each direction, slowly moving down the body, farther and farther out to the edge of the client's Hara. Allow the 11th Chakra to dissipate and fully unify with the Hara.

Move back up to the head, rotate both hands above the head, connecting into the 12th Chakra, simultaneously. Continue to rotate in each direction moving down the body, farther and farther out to the edge of the client's Hara. Allow the 12th Chakra to dissipate and fully unify with the Hara.

Completion

The practitioner then returns to the client's feet, visualizing rich iridescent neon orange earth energy flowing into the feet and up the body, flooding the bones, fascia, organs, and every cell of the body. Visualize the earth energy flowing through the Vivaxis, Hara, and all grounding connections, fully connecting them back with the planet. This step supports the client in anchoring all energetic manifestations into physical form.

Next, ask Archangel Raphael to bring sparkling iridescent green light through your hands to flood the bones, fascia, muscles, organs, and template of the body, as well as all the fields to promote healing and finalization.

As a final step, the practitioner visualizes streamers of gossamer threads woven and infused with iridescent diamonds, swirling around, and creating a three-inch-thick cocoon of energy. This protects and holds the energy allowing time to integrate and assimilate the gifts of the session.

Chapter Twenty

Axiatonal and Lightbody Integration

The Axiatonal and Lightbody Healing sequence is a healing protocol that focuses on upgrading the Lightbody to aid in our ascension and offer protections to EMF interferences that are becoming more prevalent with the introduction of higher frequency 5G technology and beyond. As we were working with the new frequencies coming in for this workshop, we realized that much of our healing work tends to focus on the physical and body-related energy fields. Thus, we often worked our way from inside to out as we worked with clients. However, we were guided in this protocol to work from the outside in.

After the essential Advanced High Frequency Shift, we move to the highest outer layers of the energy system. Transmutation on the Lightbody is then worked inward as the upgrades are integrated into the axiatonal grid system and finally into the physical. A client will receive as much as their energy system can handle at that moment in time. As the client shifts and changes, each time they will receive what is perfect for them at that moment.

The benefits of this healing protocol are as follows:

- Assists in consciously blending our own grids with the Planetary and Cosmic Grids.
- Facilitates the return of the Lightbody to its optimal attunement.
- Strengthens our connection to the Soul and Oversoul.
- Enables us to receive energy from the Universal Energy Grid.
- Helps us assimilate all aspects of self into an integrated unit.

- Adapts to the new environment, evolving the Lightbody in such a way that it does not resonate with the EMF background.

High Frequency Shift: Self

The first step of the session is Advanced High Frequency Shift (AHFS) for the practitioner. This is done while holding the feet of the client. The AHFS brings the practitioner to the optimum elevated frequency to be the conduit for the client. It also serves to entrain the client in that elevated frequency, beginning the process of healing.

High Frequency Shift: Client

The next step is to perform the client version of the AHFS, assuring the client is also at an elevated frequency.

Clearing the Outer Grids

The unique part of the protocol begins with clearing the outer four grids of the client. As explained previously, this work is done by the guides. The practitioner goes through the motions, which act to focus the intentionality and aid the work of the guides. For each pass through the grids, the practitioner visualizes passing a large hoop down the table, imagining the hoop passing on all sides of the client. The guides create special filters for the hoop for each pass. The filter is specific to the person and the particular grid being worked on by the guides.

1st grid is the Incarnation. This grid holds information related to our current incarnation assignments. Changes to this grid may clarify alignment with the client's life purpose. Aided by our guides, we make three passes of the filters through the Incarnation Grid.

2nd grid is the Soul Field Grid. First we ask the guides to help retrieve any aspects of the Soul the client may have given away. Then we ask the client to release any aspect of the Soul of others that they might be holding. It is best to ask the client out loud to release. This step alone often has a profound effect on people. As before, aided by the guides, we make three passes of the filters through the Soul Field Grid.

3rd grid is the Fascial Grid. The Fascial Grid is instrumental in multidimensional communication between the energy fields and the physical. Shifts in this grid enhance alignment and communication. As before, aided by the guides, we make three passes of the filters through the Fascia Grid.

4th grid is the DNA Grid. This grid carries familial and genetic structures. Shifts to this grid may allow old patterns to heal backward and forward in time. Again, we make three passes of the filters through the DNA Grid.

Charging Sequence

The charging sequence opens and balances the energetic body while raising the frequency and vibration of the entire field. This results in greater stabilization of the physical form to receive the work and creates a multidimensional crystalline structure that supports the transmuting and healing process. The crystalline structure serves to reinforce the grid systems. The frequency of charging defines the geometry of the crystalline structure. The crystalline structure has very noticeable differences in structure depending on the intentionality and frequency used. For this protocol, we will be utilizing the frequency of the Star Beings and the star pots. This frequency prepares the physical structure at a cellular as well as an extradimensional scale, while supporting the creation of the high frequency crystalline grid structure.

When performing this step with clients, we visualize star pots at both the foot and head of the table. We can dip into these pots and draw the metallic, yellow/orange energy from the pots into the client's body and fields. We often "see" the physical body become translucent with this material, while a multidimensional crystalline matrix is built. The client becomes a glowing multi-faceted crystal being in our hands.

We begin by moving to the foot of the table. Holding the client's feet with our thumb on the solar plexus reflex point on the bottom of the foot, visualize that you and the client are transported to a chamber before the counsel of the Ascended Masters. We ask that masters oversee this step and create an alignment with the client's life work in supporting the ascension of mankind. Invite in the Star Beings. Visualize them dipping their hands into the star pot at the base of the table and bringing that star material up into the client's feet.

At each hand position of the charging sequence, first focus on the energetic connection and star frequency flowing into the body and between your hands. Allow that energy to flood into their body, transmuting as it goes. At each hand position, we will be visualizing the creation of two triangles. One triangle points down from our hands, the apex at 10th Chakra (approximately where we are currently standing). The other triangle points up, the apex at the 8th Chakra.

At each position, invite the Star Beings to dip into the pots and spread the star material into the body where you are holding. Once the energy is connecting between your hands, visualize a triangle from your hands to a point below the feet where the 10th Chakra is located and a second triangle from your hands to the 8th Chakra above the head.

Charging Steps

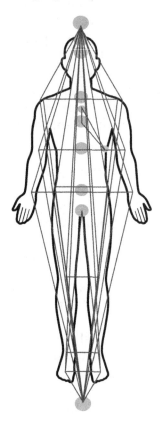

The following are the hand positions.

• Solar plexus reflex points of feet– creating triangles to 8th and 10th Chakras;

• Same position, now connect to Root Chakra and 10th Chakra.

• Both ankles – creating triangles to 8th and 10th Chakras.

• Both knees – creating triangles to 8th and 10th Chakras.

• Both hips – creating triangles to 8th and 10th Chakras.

• Both wrists – creating triangles to 8th and 10th Chakras.

• Both elbows – creating triangles to 8th and 10th Chakras.

• Hands on Spleen and Thymus, mentally connect to Heart, creating a triangle of the three points.

- Both shoulders – creating triangles to 8th and 10th Chakras
- Position right middle finger on the Brow Chakra, position left middle finger on Zeal Chakra. (at center indent point on occipital ridge) Position both thumbs on Crown Chakra. Visualize a triangle connecting these three points, activating the head centers.

Lightbody Holographic Activation

The next step involves visualization and requesting the guides to assist. We envision that a special table materializes under the client. The special table is made of clear crystal with many colored lights that shift and move in a manner that optimally works with the axiatonal spin points and Lightbody.

As the client comfortably lays on the crystal table, we approach from the right side. Slide your left hand under and behind (the back-side of) the Heart Chakra, and place your right hand at the front-side of the Heart Chakra. Settle in and attune with the zero point of the Heart Chakra. We focus our awareness into the Heart Chakra as it opens, sensing the vast extradimensional space at the zero point of the chakra.

We ask to connect with the multidimensional Oversoul and ask that the guides from all dimensional aspects of Oversoul support this work. We ask that their Lightbody be recalibrated to the highest frequency the client can integrate and hold at this time. We ask that the recalibration include the fullest activation of DNA strands.

We also ask that their Lightbody be recalibrated to the proper frequency to adapt to EMF pollution. Envision a copper frequency of sprinkles/dust flowing into the holograph which gets woven into the gridwork to protect and transmute EMF and 5G frequencies.

Hold as the holographic Lightbody template is recalibrated. This step could take a few minutes. We continue to hold the highest frequency possible and wait for a sense of completion.

Resetting Outer Gridwork

Aided by our guides, we will be using filters to reset the outer grids. This is similar to the gridwork steps at the beginning of the protocol, however only one pass through each grid is required. In addition, the Star Beings will be assisting and bringing the energy of the star pots into each filter as the grid is reset.

First, dip the filter into the star pots at the head of the table, inviting the Star Beings, then move the filter through the grids.

1st pass is the Incarnation Grid, use one pass of the filter.

Dip again into the star pot.

2nd pass is the Soul Field Grid, use one pass of the filter.

Dip again into the star pot.

3rd pass is the Fascial Grid, use one pass of the filter.

Dip again into the star pot.

4th pass is the DNA Grid to reset the upgraded new structures, use one pass of the filter.

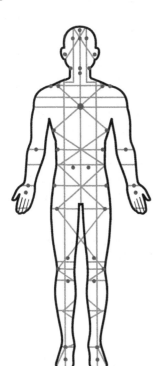

Dip your fingers into the star pot at the end of the table and sweep back up through the body, spreading the star frequency through the entire physical body and fields.

Activation of Vertical Lines and Spin Points

This next step activates the spin points and vertical structures assisting the energetic step-down of the high Lightbody frequency into the lower energetic frequency of the physical form.

Sweep hands together, palms off the body, across the center of the head. At shoulders, split hands, sweeping over each shoulder and down each arm, off the fingers.

Next pass sweep hands together over the center of head and torso down to hips. At hips, hands separate, sweeping across each hip, down each leg, off the feet.

3rd pass, sweep down the centerline of the head and body, between the legs and off the feet below the table.

Repeat this sequence 3x This is activating all the spin points.

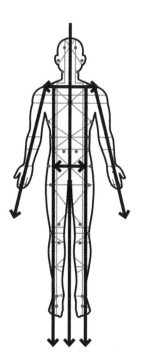

Linking Up the Grids of the Lightbody

Next step in the step-down sequence is to link up the grids with the Lightbody. Star/ Galactic Beings facilitate this through our etheric fingers. This activates the spin points that weave interdimensionally, weaving through all the grids at each of the eight points around the body. Our intentionality to connect is important, as we are not specifically connecting to each of the thousands of spin points.

Draw a double figure 8 pattern down from above, crossing in the Incarnation Grid, crossing again in the Soul Field Grid, cross next the Fascia Grid, lastly cross in the DNA grid, anchoring each grid into the Spin Points in the body.

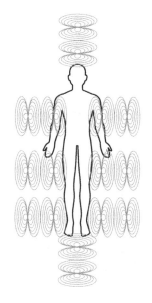

Repeat this sequence (from the top of the table 2 more times, 3 positions at right side of the table, 3x each position, foot of the table 3x, moving to the left side of the table 3 positions at, 3x each position. See above diagram).

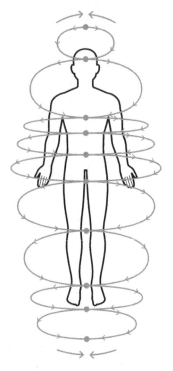

Activating the Orion Helix

Using both hands, above the body, we slowly trace the arcs in the shape of the helix. As we move down the body our hands cross nine times.

Starting at Soul Star (9th Chakra), trace a series of ellipses, crossing hands at: brow, heart, solar plexus, navel, root, knees, ankles, bottom of feet, Earth Star (10th Chakra).

Retrace the helix back up from Earth Star to Soul Star, again crossing nine times.

Repeat up AND down two more times for a total of three cycles.

Completion

The practitioner then returns to the client's feet, visualizing rich iridescent neon orange earth energy flowing into the feet and up the body, flooding the bones, fascia, organs, and every cell of the body. Visualize the earth energy flowing through the Vivaxis, Hara, and all grounding connections, fully connecting them back with the planet. This step supports the client in anchoring all energetic manifestations into physical form.

Next, ask Archangel Raphael to bring sparkling iridescent green light through your hands to flood the bones, fascia, muscles, organs, and template of the body, as well as all the fields to promote healing and finalization.

As a final step, the practitioner visualizes streamers of gossamer threads woven and infused with iridescent diamonds, swirling around, and creating a three-inch-thick cocoon of energy. This protects and holds the energy allowing time to integrate and assimilate the gifts of the session.

Chapter Twenty-one

Neural Reset and DNA Activation

This protocol stems from neuroplasticity healing work that Jeannette did many years earlier with children struggling with learning challenges. Working with these frequencies helps to reorganize the neural networks in the brain to heal and stabilize.

As usual, the three of us all began experimenting with and adapting this protocol by bringing in additional supporting frequencies for ourselves, as well as our clients. This protocol has been shifted into a higher frequency and comes from that guidance and refinement in practice.

The purpose of this technique is to:

- Shift the ability of the brain's neural networks to change through growth and reorganization.
- Activate the brain cells to communicate with one another to form and reform new connections.
- Heal, change, and rewire traumas (including brain injuries and strokes).
- Realign, reconnect, and activate the additional 10 strands of DNA within the neurological network, allowing us to live in multidimensional consciousness.
- Align each strand of DNA to connect to different aspects of the chakras and our neural pathways.
- Embrace the next stage of our energy body evolution.

High Frequency Shift: Self

The first step of the session is Advanced High Frequency Shift (AHFS) for the practitioner. This is done while holding the feet of the client. The AHFS brings the practitioner to the optimum elevated frequency to be the conduit for the client. It also serves to entrain the client in that elevated frequency, beginning the process of healing.

High Frequency Shift: Client

The next step is to perform the client version of the AHFS, assuring the client is also at an elevated frequency.

Gabriel's Clearing and Toroidal Field Clearing

The practitioner comes around to the client's right/right side of the table and slides their hands under the client. One hand is placed behind the heart, and the other goes under the pelvis or sacrum. Archangel Gabriel and her helpers are invited to support the client. Invite the client to visualize that they are floating in a pool of warm golden fluid.

Gently move your hands to create the motion of being swirled from side to side in the golden fluid. Allow the golden fluid to nurture them and release any anxieties. Continue the movement for a few minutes. The client stays floating in the pool as the practitioner shifts to a gentle vibration using the hand under the pelvis to create soft vibrations, like ripples in the pool. Let the ripples release and cleanse. Slowly move the vibrations up the lumbar spine to the thoracic spine, and finally up to the base of the head, releasing tension as the vibration moves up the back. Allow this to occur for a few minutes. Next, switch back to the motion of swirling from side to side for about another minute. When this feels complete, gently slide your hands out to work with the toroidal fields.

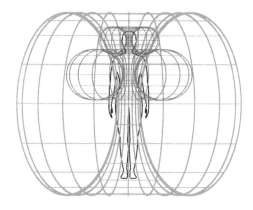

Using etheric fingers dripping with the warm golden fluid. Clear and align the toroidal field of the body by gently following the toroidal lines from above the head, down to the feet on the outside of the field, then back up the middle. Do this 3–5 times.

Repeat the tracing of the toroidal field pattern around the heart torus.

Do this 3–5 times.

Repeat the tracing of the toroidal field pattern around the brain torus.

Do this 3–5 times.

Uriel's Infusing and DNA Activation

The practitioner moves to the top of the table and softly places one hand on each side of the client's head, palms against the temples. Invite Archangel Uriel and her helpers to bring their healing energy. As the client is held, Uriel begins to infuse the brain with her brilliant gold-white energy.

Visualize that energy expanding through the brain. Allow the energy to flow down the spinal cord and out to each part of the body via the nervous system. Ask that the golden-white energy flow into each cell, allowing it to integrate with and energize the DNA.

Auric Field Clearing

Moving to the client's feet, Uriel's golden energy is used to clear the first four layers of the auric field. The practitioner uses both hands together to slowly start building a clockwise vortex of energy at 10th Chakra. As the golden vortex energy grows, invite in the Comet Beings to assist. They invigorate the vortex as it spins faster, while the focus is kept on the etheric layer of the aura. When the energy vortex feels strong, spiral up the body towards the head, then off the table.

Repeat the process again starting at 10th Chakra, creating the golden vortex with the Comet Beings. Focus on clearing the vortex through the emotional layer of the aura.

Come back to the foot and create another golden vortex with the Comet Beings at the 10th Chakra. Focus on clearing the vortex through the mental layer of the aura.

Again, from the 10th Chakra, create the golden vortex with the Comet Beings and clear it through the spiritual layer of the aura.

Archangel Michael's Neural Infusion

The practitioner moves to the top of the table and places the thumbs over the fontanel (top of head where bone plates join, the soft spot on an infant's head), cupping the top of the client's head in their palms. Archangel Michael is invited to assist with his neural infusion. While holding the client's head, visualize Archangel Michael's electric cobalt blue light flowing from the palms and fingers. Allow the blue light to infuse and energize all the nerve cells in the brain.

Visualize it integrating with the gold from Uriel's neural infusion, illuminating, energizing, and resetting all the neurons in the brain with electric cobalt blue. Hold this position for several minutes until the infusion feels complete.

The practitioner moves their hands so that the fingers are on each side of the occipital ridge, with fingers pointed down toward the neck. The back of the client's brain (the occipital lobe) will be in the palms. Visualize the electric cobalt blue light flowing from the brain and brain stem down the neck via the 12 cranial nerves. Visualize the light spreading through the nervous system, down and throughout the entire body to the feet.

Hold this position until the entire nervous system is filled with and integrates the gold and cobalt blue. When it feels complete, gently place the palms over the client's eyes and hold for about one minute to complete integration.

Floating with Raguel and the Dolphins

The practitioner moves to the side of the table and slides their hands under the client, placing them behind the heart and under the pelvis. Ask the client to invite Archangel Raguel and the dolphins and to imagine they are floating in a beautiful aqua blue pool, visualizing the dolphins circling around them in the pool. Slowly rock the client to create the sensation of floating in the pool with the dolphins.

As the dolphins circle the client, ask Raguel and the dolphins to harmonize their sounds so the client's relationship with self and the Creator is restored to Divine balance of peace and harmony. The practitioner may be intuitively drawn to tone with the dolphins. Continue to hold the client in the aqua blue pool for a few minutes to allow for stabilization of the treatment, while setting the intention to infuse them with joy and hope.

Completion

As a final step, the practitioner visualizes streamers of gossamer threads woven and infused with iridescent diamonds, swirling around, and creating a three-inch-thick cocoon of energy. This protects and holds the energy allowing time to integrate and assimilate the gifts of the session.

Chapter Twenty-two

Matrix Quantum Healing

The Matrix Quantum Healing sequence is a complete healing sequence that embodies most of the teachings of the workshop. This is typical for our workshops. In some of the previous workshops, we were downloaded the entire final healing sequence first, then we had to figure out how to teach the parts to create the whole. This workshop was built in a different pattern as the final sequence did not totally solidify until near the end of our planning phase. As such, this sequence will bring in elements of previous protocols.

This protocol can be used with clients with or without building up to it with all the pieces. We teach it in pieces as it would be a bit too much for the participant to assimilate at one time. A client that has not experienced some of the preceding elements will receive as much as their energy system can handle at that moment in time. It can be repeated multiple times on self or clients as they will be changing and transforming. Each time the energy will shift as the person is ready to receive and evolve.

The benefits of this healing protocol are as follows:

- Facilitates optimal attunement of the Lightbody Hologram. The protocol works with the multidimensions of the Soul, Oversoul, and Core Essence. The Lightbody Hologram gets restructured to the highest possible frequencies that can be held at the time of the protocol.

- Strengthens our connection to the Soul and Oversoul by activation of the 12 Rays of Light. The protocol includes activation of the 12 Rays. The Rays will deepen and enhance the connections to Soul and Oversoul. Those Rays that can work to the highest good at this moment will activate and aid in the integration of the healing work.

- Creates Sonic and Light ripples multidimensionally to transmute and heal past, present, and future. This protocol works multidimensionally through all mediums that affect the energetic system. Healing can be done forward and backward in time, as time is an illusion when we are operating beyond the limitations of 3D reality.

- Quantumly encodes the 12 Strands of DNA. The Lightbody recalibration includes activation of all twelve strands of DNA. The sequence includes the use of Primary Cell as a step-down process to allow encoding the triple helix DNA patterns from Lightbody into the physical body.

- Unifies the Hara with the 12 chakras to support assimilation of all aspects of the self into an integrated unit. Use of the Advanced High Frequency Shift unifies the chakras and Hara of both practitioner and client. This unification allows cohesive functioning of chakra systems into a more integrated whole.

- Links Head and Heart. An element of the mind clearance protocol is brought in to link head and heart, moving our awareness out of the head and into our heart. It also softens brain wiring related to drama and trauma, reducing the focus on "the story" and shifting to the loving lessons.

- Enables us to receive energy from the Universal Energy Grid. This protocol upgrades and clears the entire human energy system. The newly tuned up energy system will more effectively receive and integrate universal energy.

- Adapts to the new environment, evolving the Lightbody in such a way that it does not resonate with the EMF background. EMF continues to grow in our technological world. This protocol includes elements to help shift the Lightbody into frequencies that are less susceptible to EMF interference. It also includes steps to build protection into the Lightbody and physical body.

Workshop Experiential

This exercise is done as an energy healing trade. Participants pair up. One assumes the role of the practitioner, the other the role of the client or recipient of the work. After the session is complete and time is taken for discussion and reflection, the participants reverse roles so that both have an opportunity to give and receive.

Our intentionality is set for our client's highest good at this time in their life journey. This is guided work, so we ask for the highest frequency level of guidance needed to help the client today. This sequence has a number of steps, so it is best to have printed materials to help when first practicing, until the practitioner can do it from memory.

High Frequency Shift: Self

The first step of the session is Advanced High Frequency Shift (AHFS) for the practitioner. This is done while holding the feet of the client. The AHFS brings the practitioner to the optimum elevated frequency to be the conduit for the client. It also serves to entrain the client in that elevated frequency, beginning the process of healing.

High Frequency Shift: Client

The next step is to perform the client version of the AHFS, assuring the client is also at an elevated frequency.

Clearing the Outer Grids

The unique part of the protocol begins with clearing the outer four grids of the client. As explained previously, this work is done by the guides. The practitioner goes through the motions, which act to focus the intentionality and aid the work of the guides. For each pass through the grids, the practitioner visualizes passing a large hoop down the table, imagining the hoop passing on all sides of the client. The guides create special filters for the hoop for each pass. The filter is specific to the person and the particular grid being worked on by the guides.

1st grid is the Incarnation. This grid holds information related to our current incarnation assignments. Changes to this grid may clarify alignment with the client's life purpose. Aided by our guides, we make three passes of the filters through the Incarnation Grid.

2nd is the Soul Field Grid. First we ask the guides to help retrieve any aspects of the Soul the client may have given away. Then we ask the client to release any aspect of the Soul of others that they might be holding. It is best to ask the client out loud to release. This step alone often has a profound effect on people. As before, aided by the guides, we make three passes of the filters through the Soul Field Grid.

3rd grid is the Fascia grid. Fascial Grid is instrumental in multidimensional communication between the energy fields and the physical. Shifts in this grid enhance the alignment and communication. As before, aided by the guides, we make three passes of the filters through the Fascia grid.

4th grid is the DNA grid. This grid carries familial and genetic structures. Shifts to this grid may allow old patterns to heal backwards and forward in time. Again, three passes of the filters through the DNA grid.

Charging sequence

The charging sequence opens and balances the energetic body while raising the frequency and vibration of the entire field. This results in greater stabilization of the physical form to receive the work and creates a multidimensional crystalline structure that supports the transmuting and healing process. The crystalline structure serves to reinforce the grid systems. The frequency of charging defines the geometry of the crystalline structure. The crystalline structure has very noticeable differences in structure depending on the intentionality and frequency used. For this protocol, we will be utilizing the frequency of the Star Beings and the star pots. This frequency prepares the physical structure at a cellular as well as an extradimensional scale, while supporting the creation of the high frequency crystalline grid structure.

When performing this step with clients, we visualize star pots at both the foot and head of the table. We can dip into these pots and draw the metallic, yellow/orange energy from the pots into the client's body and fields. We often "see" the physical body become translucent with this material, while a multidimensional crystalline matrix is built. The client becomes a glowing multi-faceted crystal being in our hands.

We begin by moving to the foot of the table. Holding the client's feet with our thumb on the solar plexus reflex point on the bottom of the foot, visualize that you and the client are transported to a chamber before the counsel of the Ascended Masters. We ask that masters oversee this step and create an alignment with the client's life work in supporting the ascension of mankind. Invite in the Star Beings. Visualize them dipping their hands into the star pot at the base of the table and bringing that star material up into the client's feet.

At each hand position of the charging sequence, first focus on the energetic connection and star frequency flowing into the body and between your hands. Allow that energy to flood into their body, transmuting as it goes. At each hand position, we will be visualizing the creation of two triangles. One triangle points down from our hands, the apex at 10th Chakra (approximately where we are currently standing). The other triangle points up, the apex at the 8th Chakra.

At each position, invite the Star Beings to dip into the pots and spread the star material into the body where you are holding. Once the energy is connecting between your hands, visualize a triangle from your hands to a point below the feet where the 10th Chakra is located and a second triangle from your hands to the 8th Chakra above the head.

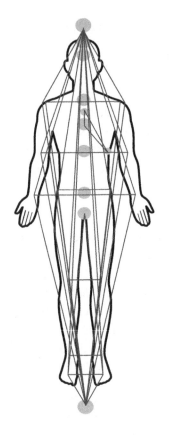

Charging Steps

The following are the hand positions.

• Solar plexus reflex points of feet – creating triangles to 8ᵗʰ and 10ᵗʰ Chakras;

• Same position, now connect to Root Chakra and 10ᵗʰ Chakra.

• Both ankles – creating triangles to 8th and 10ᵗʰ Chakras.

• Both knees – creating triangles to 8ᵗʰ and 10ᵗʰ Chakras.

• Both hips – creating triangles to 8ᵗʰ and 10ᵗʰ Chakras.

• Both wrists – creating triangles to 8th and 10ᵗʰ Chakras.

• Both elbows – creating triangles to 8ᵗʰ and 10ᵗʰ Chakras.

• Hands on Spleen and Thymus, mentally connect to Heart, creating a triangle of the three points.

• Both shoulders – creating triangles to 8ᵗʰ and 10ᵗʰ Chakras

• Position right middle finger on the Brow Chakra, position left middle finger on Zeal Chakra. (at center indent point on occipital ridge) Position both thumbs on Crown Chakra. Visualize a triangle connecting these three points, activating the head centers.

Lightbody Holographic Activation

The next step involves visualization and requesting the guides to assist. We envision that a special table materializes under the client. The special table is made of clear crystal with many colored lights that shift and move in a manner that optimally works with the axiatonal spin points and Lightbody.

As the client comfortably lays on the crystal table, we approach from the right side. Slide your left hand under and behind (the back-side of) the Heart Chakra, and place your right hand at the front-side of the Heart Chakra. Settle in and attune with the zero point of the Heart Chakra. We focus our awareness into the Heart Chakra as it opens, sensing the vast extradimensional space at the zero point of the chakra.

We ask to connect with the multidimensional Oversoul and ask that the guides from all dimensional aspects of Oversoul support this work. We ask that their Lightbody be recalibrated to the highest frequency the client can integrate and hold at this time. We ask that the recalibration include the fullest activation of DNA strands.

We also ask that their Lightbody be recalibrated to the proper frequency to adapt to EMF pollution. Envision a copper frequency of sprinkles/ dust flowing into the holograph which gets woven into the gridwork to protect and transmute EMF and 5G frequencies.

Hold as the holographic Lightbody template is recalibrated. This step could take a few minutes. We continue to hold the highest frequency possible and wait for a sense of completion.

Resetting Outer Gridwork

Aided by our guides, we will be using filters to reset the outer grids. This is similar to the gridwork steps at the beginning of the protocol, however only one pass through each grid is required. In addition, the Star Beings will be assisting and bringing the energy of the star pots into each filter as the grid is reset.

First, dip the filter into the star pots at the head of the table, inviting the Star Beings, then move the filter through the grids.

1st pass is the Incarnation Grid, use one pass of the filter.

Dip again into the star pot.

2nd pass is the Soul Field Grid, use one pass of the filter.

Dip again into the star pot.

3rd pass is the Fascial Grid, use one pass of the filter.

Dip again into the star pot.

4th pass is the DNA grid to reset the upgraded new structures, use one pass of the filter.

Dip your fingers into the star pot at the end of the table and sweep back up through the body, spreading the star frequency through the entire physical body and fields.

Activation of Vertical Lines and Spin Points

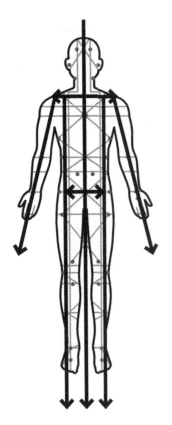

This next step activates the spin points and vertical structures assisting step-down of the Lightbody high frequency energy into the lower frequency of the physical form:

Sweep hands together, palms off the body, across the center of the head. At shoulders, split hands, sweeping over each shoulder and down each arm, off the fingers.

Next pass sweep hands together over the center of head and torso down to hips. At hips, hands separate, sweeping across each hip, down each leg, off the feet.

3rd pass, sweep down the centerline of the head and body, between the legs and off the feet below the table.

Repeat this sequence 3x This is activating all the spin points.

Linking Up the Grids of the Lightbody

Next step in the step-down sequence is to link up the grids with the Lightbody. Star/Galactic Beings facilitate this through our etheric fingers. This activates the spin points that weave interdimensionally, weaving through all the grids at each of the eight points around the body. Our intentionality to connect is important, as we are not specifically connecting to each of the thousands of spin points.

Draw a double figure 8 pattern down from above, crossing in the Incarnation Grid, crossing again in the Soul Field Grid, cross next the Fascial Grid, lastly cross in the DNA Grid, anchoring each grid into the Spin Points in the body.

Repeat this sequence (from the top of the table 2 more times, 3 positions at right side of the table, 3x each position, foot of the table 3x, moving to the left side of the table 3 positions at, 3x each position).

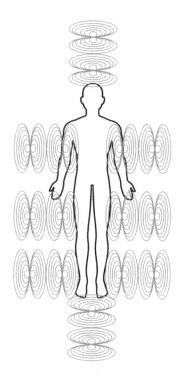

Activating the Orion Helix

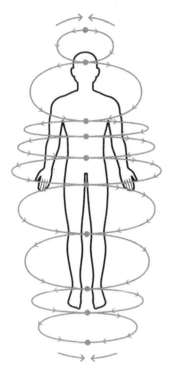

Using both hands, above the body, we slowly trace the arcs in the shape of the helix. As we move down the body our hands cross nine times.

Starting at Soul Star (9th Chakra), trace a series of ellipses, crossing hands at: brow, heart, solar plexus, navel, root, knees, ankles, bottom of feet, Earth Star (10th Chakra).

Retrace the helix back up from Earth Star to Soul Star, again crossing nine times.

Repeat up AND down two more times for a total of three cycles.

Primary Cell Activation of 12 Strands of DNA

This step works with the Primary Cell to facilitate a step-down of the DNA activation from the Lightbody into the DNA of the physical body. The practitioner moves to the right side of the treatment table, placing one hand on the heart and one hand on the high heart, connecting deeply at their heart and Soul level.

Next the practitioner brings their hands together above the client's heart, with open palms facing up. The Primary Cell is invited into the open palms. If the Primary Cell appears as restricted or inactive, ask that it open and be receptive to new information. It has always opened to such a request for us.

When the Primary Cell is open and ready, invite in the 12 Rays of Light. Your intention is to support the qualities of each Ray to fill the Primary Cell and client at the highest frequency they are ready to receive.

Ask that the Primary Cell open to the new frequencies of the DNA, three strands at a time. The new Lightbody activations get brought into the Primary Cell DNA, allowing triple helix formation and full utilization of existing DNA material.

When the first three-strand activation seems complete, ask the second set of three strands to activate. Repeat this process two more times, allowing all twelve strands of DNA to be activated.

Primary Cell Infusion into Heart

Before the Primary Cell is infused into the heart, we pause to allow the client's Core Essence to connect and come to full resonance with the physical heart. Allow the Heart Chakra and physical heart to take in the frequency of the client's Core Essence and resonate with that frequency.

Then, the practitioner opens their hands and returns the Primary Cell back to the body. Visualize the revitalized Primary Cell merge with the heart and fuse the new genetic imprint into the heart tissues. We will often sense this as waves of energy going out like ripples in a pond. As the Primary Cell fuses, visualize the link-up of energy between the Core Essence, heart, and 8th Chakra.

Expansion and Propagation through Fascia

Continue the propagation of the new genetic imprint and frequency as the Primary Cell is being fused into the fascia of the heart.

Using breath, visualize breathing in and expanding the heart, expanding the fascia, and breaking old restrictions, allowing space for expansion and change.

Continue that expansion, and using the breath, visualize the new genetic imprint and frequency of the heart fascia spreading through the body. Breathe it first into the upper chest, then the neck, head, back, right arm to fingers, left arm to fingers, torso, right leg to toes, and left leg to toes. Feel the entire fascia system light up with the new frequency, free and elastic. Through the fascia allow the new DNA imprint to spread to every cell in the client's body.

Mind Clearance, Oversoul Connection and Neural Stimulation

The practitioner next moves to the top of the table. We use the last hand positions from the Mind Clearance protocol (Chapter 18). Place your left arm so that your hand is near the Heart Chakra (with appropriate touch) and the client's head is resting on your forearm. The practitioner's right hand cups the right side of the client's skull, with thumb pointing toward the Crown Chakra.

Pause in this position to sense the undulating energy flowing between the hands as the heart and head connect. Invite the client's Oversoul to fully connect with their Soul and Heart Chakra. Allow balance and full integration as a weaving of these aspects, Heart (the will), High Heart (Soul), and the Oversoul.

Visualize Archangel Michael's electric cobalt blue light flowing from the right hand into the head. Allow it to infuse and energize all the nerve cells in the brain. The golden light of Uriel's infusion follows from the right hand, weaving with the blue, creating a blue/gold neural infusion, illuminating, energizing, and resetting all the neurons in the brain.

Visualize that electric cobalt blue light, woven with golden strands flowing from the brain stem, spreading down and throughout the body to the feet. Hold until the entire nervous system is filled with gold and cobalt blue.

DNA Protection

The next step brings a gift to provide DNA protection to block out any backdoor entrances or hacks to the DNA that may have been encoded in the past. The practitioner stands alongside the table, hands outstretched, visualizing an 8-sided star in the palm of their hand. The star is a clear crystalline form. As it is held, it shatters into billions of tiny 8-sided stars. The shower of micro stars floats down into the body, into every cell.

Zip up

Next step is "zipping up the field". This is done starting with holding the palms of both hands on the soles of the feet. The practitioner holds each position for about 15–20 seconds, allowing the energy to flow, with the intention of sealing in the work. Work your way up the body "zipping" in the sequence listed below.

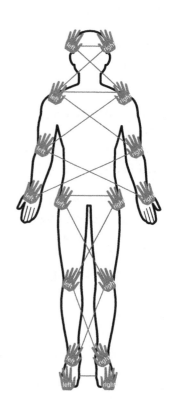

15. Hands on bottom of feet.

16. Left ankle and right knee.

17. Right ankle and left knee.

18. Left knee and right hip.

19. Right knee and left hip.

20. Both hips.

21. Left wrist and right elbow.

22. Right wrist and left elbow.

23. Left elbow and right shoulder.

24. Right elbow and left shoulder.

25. Both shoulders.

26. Left shoulder and right side of the head.

27. Right shoulder and left side of the head.

28. Both sides of the head.

Completion

The practitioner then returns to the client's feet, visualizing rich iridescent neon orange earth energy flowing into the feet and up the body, flooding the bones, fascia, organs, and every cell of the body. Visualize the earth energy flowing through the Vivaxis, Hara, and all grounding connections, fully connecting them back with the planet. This step supports the client in anchoring all energetic manifestations into physical form.

Next, ask Archangel Raphael to bring sparkling iridescent green light through your hands to flood the bones, fascia, muscles, organs, and template of the body, as well as all the fields to promote healing and finalization.

As a final step, the practitioner visualizes streamers of gossamer threads woven and infused with iridescent diamonds, swirling around, and creating a three-inch-thick cocoon of energy. This protects and holds the energy allowing time to integrate and assimilate the gifts of the session.

Chapter Twenty-three

Closing Invocation: October 2020

We finish the workshop in ceremony, using the following invocation to reinforce the learning and help set the new frequencies as the participants return to their normal lives. The ceremony included a ritual to cement their bond as a group and commit to global service.

Amplifying Higher Frequencies: Greater Alignment with Divine Consciousness

I am fused with the new Earth, in fluid motion with the crystalline matrix of the earth, and my awareness expands.

I am connected here with the elements, the minerals, and earth grids.

I bow in honor to the ancestors and elemental beings and guides protecting this space.

I am transmuted and flow with the Earth, Stars, Moon, and the Galaxy; I am healed and whole.

I am breath and the expansive energy of life; my entire being is flowing with the Rays of Light.

I am a fully purified holographic beacon of Light, one with the energy flowing from Spirit.

I am a Radiant Being, my activated DNA fully embracing the Divine Light.

I delight in my quantum existence, feeling the wonder, expansion, and Matrix of love.

I vow to serve the Divine plan, holding the highest possible frequencies.

I bring forth the expanded expression of my unified Lightbody.

I embody and bridge all possibilities of healing and planetary service.

I am awake and Divine, and I revel in my Divinity.

Conclusion

Final Notes

It is our wish that the work that we have shared supports the evolution of humankind, by contributing to the collective of Lightworkers on planet earth and connecting to the vast consciousness of Light Beings that are ever-present for us to raise all Souls to even higher frequencies.

We know that this work is one of many paths that the supporting guides use to bring in the new frequencies to earth in support of our common evolution. We hope that each of these paths merge into a clear road for mankind to find its way home.

We realize that we are but a small group that holds this high frequency of light for the collective, but fully trust that we each make a difference in this evolution. Our intention is to create a collection of web-based content to support the material in this book. Our hope is that it enables all types of learners to access the material, leading to broader sharing of the highest possible frequencies.

Tim and Franny

Appendix

Glossary

Advanced High Frequency Shift: (AHFS) An updated and more detailed exercise to train your energy system to access more of the highest available frequencies and prepare for the more advanced energies as our evolution continues.

Angels: Spiritual beings that act as messengers or agents of the Divine. Available to assist us when asked. It is thought we are always surrounded by angels and each of us has one or more guardian angels.

Ascended Masters: A spiritual being that was once in human form, mastered ascension, and karmically not required to incarnate. Part of the team of spiritual beings assisting humanity to evolve and ascend.

Ascension: The process of ascending to a higher spiritual level, level of enlightenment, or higher state of consciousness.

Axiatonal Grid: Axia = axis or direction; Tonal = sound or vibration; Electrical in nature, The Axiatonal Grid combines color and sound to realign blood, lymph, and the nervous system, into Divine template. The Axiatonal meridian system is part of the step-down process from Lightbody to physical body. Equivalent of acupuncture meridians but connecting the Oversoul and resonant star systems with the physical. Through the Axiatonal lines, the gridwork of Lightbody is translated into programming of the human body.

Basic High Frequency Shift: (BHFS) Exercise is foundational to training your energy system to access available frequencies and prepare for the more advanced energies now coming through.

Consciousness: The awareness of self and one's surroundings.

Core Essence: Is your Light, the Divine spark of God that you are now, have been, and always will be. The position of Core Essence is the current expression of the frequency you are in this physical dimension. It also embodies the frequencies which reflect or represent other aspects of you.

Empath: A highly sensitive person with an ability to sense, experience or take on the thoughts, feelings, emotions or physical pain of those around them. Many empaths experience these sensations, yet have trouble discerning the origin of the sensation.

Energy Therapy: A therapy (there are many versions) where a trained practitioner consciously works with the human energy field and energy matrix of a client to restore balance and harmony.

Extradimensional: Originating and operating outside the known physical three-dimensional physical reality. Working in many dimensions beyond the normal 3D of time and space.

Flower of Life: Sacred geometry form, at least 6,000 years old. Contains fundamental forms of time and space. We use it as protection and as a vehicle.

Frequency: In electromagnetics, it refers to the numbers of waves that pass a fixed place in a given amount of time. So, it is basically the rate of vibration.

Guardians: Spiritual beings that serve a role as protector, sentinel, or defender.

Guides: Our team of Spirits (usually disincarnate) that serve to teach, guide, and protect us.

Hara: Column of energy we incarnate on and our intentions of life purpose create an energetic connection from Spirit to form on this planet. Hara has an internal structure and an external structure.

High Frequency: Heightened levels of energetic awareness and existence. When in a state of high frequency, the human energy system functions at a more optimum state and has greater awareness of higher levels of consciousness.

Holograph: In our 3D world, a Hologram is a projection of a light field as an interference pattern that creates a light field. That field produces an accurate reproduction of the original image such that it can be viewed from different angles and creates the illusion of a true 3D object. Our usage of the term is from the perspective of a multi-dimensional reality where projections into the Matrix from many dimensions creates holographic fields which carry organizing energies and can be perceived by some sensitive people.

Lightbody: A holographic projection upon the Matrix, comprising many organizing fields. These fields define our spiritual and physical manifestation in this world.

Merkaba: Considered to be a Lightbody vehicle used to connect with and reach higher frequencies. It also is known to be multidimensional, allowing access to the other planes. It is used as a tool by Archangel Metatron.

Metatron's Cube: A representation of how energy flows through the Universe. It contains all Platonic Solids also holding 13 circles within. It is used as a cleansing device.

Oversoul: The primordial or highest level of Soul, where it retains both the properties of being the self as well as being the selfless one.

Quantum: Properly defined as the smallest unit of many forms of energy. At the smallest of scales of quantum physics, the rules of interaction become different from classic physics. Our use of the term refers to complex interdimensional interactions of energy at this smallest scale.

Rays or Ray of Light: A title for a specific or focused consciousness of the Creator. In this usage, light is information. Each Ray is already part of our Soul waiting to emerge. The Rays are a form of teaching this information, they are a Spiritual School of Light.

Vibration: An oscillation or movement of a fluid, elastic solid, or medium, or an electromagnetic wave.

Vivaxis ("Axis of Life"): Your own personal generator in the energy field into which you are born. Formed within a few weeks of your birth. An agreement between the Earth and the Soul that will support what you came here to do in this lifetime.

Bibliography

Bailey, A. A. (1953). *Esoteric Healing.* Lucis Publishing Company.

Brennan, B. A. (1993). *Light Emerging: The Journey of Personal Healing.* Bantam Books.

Dale, C. (2009). *The Subtle Body: An Encyclopedia of Your Energetic Anatomy.* Sounds True Inc.

Dale, C. (2010). *The Complete Book of Chakra Healing* (2nd ed.). Llewellyn Publications.

Glasson, N. S. (2010). *The Twelve Rays of Light.* Derwen Publishing.

Hovland, S. (2000). *Vibratory Grid Activation.*

Nienaber, J. M. (2019). *The Heart in You: A Personal Journey through Your Physical, Emotional, Mental and Spiritual Heart.* Balboa Press.

Noël, R. (2011). *The Huggin' Healer.* Publish America.

Jacka, J. (2000). *The Vivaxis Connection: Healing Through Earth Energies.* Hampton Roads Publishing.

Mcfetridge, G. (2004). *Peak States of Consciousness: Theory and Application.* Institute For the Study of Peak States Press.

About the Authors

After working together for several years, Tim McConville and Franny Harcey were divinely guided to share their collective wisdom, and Awakening Healing Axis was born. Through the synergy of their collaboration, they have found it possible to go much deeper into the work of personal healing and supporting others in their quest for self-healing and transformation. With individual backgrounds in various energy modalities, Tim and Franny have created work that focuses on raising their collective frequency and those they share with, in order to contribute to the ascension of human consciousness.

This unique approach incorporates new healing techniques, increasing our understanding of the science supporting energy therapies while linking to the development of new insights among esoteric healing, human physiology, and energy therapy through the multi-dimensional bio fields. Offering retreats throughout the year, Awakening Healing Axis uses natural settings to create a foundation for sharing their work, thereby inviting participants to experience greater depths of personal exploration. To learn more, please visit awakeninghealingaxis.com

Made in the USA
Monee, IL
01 April 2022

93593622R00095